6695348
940.548

Hertfordshire
COUNTY COUNCIL
Community Information

L32a

Please renew/return this item by the last date shown.

So that your telephone call is charged at local rate, please call the numbers as set out below:

	From Area codes 01923 or 0208:	From the rest of Herts:
Renewals:	01923 471373	01438 737373
Enquiries:	01923 471333	01438 737333
Minicom:	01923 471599	01438 737599

L32b

D1634135

Uncertain Wings

Uncertain Wings

The Duchess of St Albans

W. H. ALLEN · LONDON
A Howard & Wyndham Company
1977

For Clare

Foreword

Let it be clearly understood that this is in no way a history of the campaign in the Mediterranean theatre during the last war. Strictly forbidden to keep a diary as we were, I have had to describe events as I understood, or misunderstood them at the time. It is solely a worm's eye view, packed with misconceptions, immature deductions, prejudice and 'passionate squeaks', as my husband describes even the mildest of my protests against injustice.

And if I appear at times prudish, prim and prissy, I was more than likely exactly that. But I make no excuses. One is what one is, et voilà tout.

My gratitude goes to my husband for reading the manuscript and checking facts and dates, and toning down some of my most misguided assumptions; to Miss Tania Wolff for making my task easier by preserving all my wartime letters, and to Mary, Princess of Pless, for tirelessly winkling out invaluable books of reference, and to Mr Leonard Mosley for constant encouragement and advice.

I

When my grand-daughter was two and half, she said to me one fine morning as we sat together in the garden of the Mas Mistral, my childhood home in the South of France as far back as I can remember, 'When Clare was a little girl, (and she indicated the size of a matchstick with her two forefingers) Mummy used to give her drinks of milk from her bosom. Can Clare have a little snack out of *your* bosom, Grandma?'

Well, that one was simple enough to deal with, but when the time comes for her to say, 'And what did *you* do in the war, Grandma?' it will not be an easy matter to answer the question with much conviction, nor to justify my various doings as being of much use to anyone. Our childhood friends were all either trapped in France by the occupying forces, or in the Guards, or in the infantry, or driving tanks, bombers or Spitfires, motor torpedo boats, and various other engines of war. And when I think of my brother John parachuting out of the Normandy sky, and bashing his way up to Germany with hardly a scratch, and sister Anne battling single-handed on the night shift in her Australian hospital, with lecherous one-legged old men, whose wooden limbs had to be locked up in the medicine cupboard to restrain their bottom-pinching activities, my own contribution to the war seems less impressive still.

Even so, it was rather deflating when, several years later, on meeting a Special Operations Executive character who had been operating with the Partisans in the wilds of Jugoslavia where Evelyn Waugh, Randolph Churchill and others of that ilk had conducted their eccentric and high-spirited, top-secret activities, I asked him to what purpose they had put the news digests over which I had slogged for so many long, steaming hot nights, and received the light-hearted rejoinder: 'So it was *you* who sent us all that useless bumf? Well, my dear, if you want to know the truth, I dumped it straight into the waste-paper basket the minute it arrived.'

On the whole, it was all rather nebulous. I floated through a large part of the war in a kind of dream, mostly pleasant, I must say, and when less so, suffered as philosophically as possible until better times returned. There were of course moments of seething rage and bitter indignation against the enemy, but that was mostly where personal issues were involved, and my family were in the firing line, and getting what I considered more than their fair share of war damage. Not, perhaps, a very worthy attitude when you are supposed to be fighting the forces of darkness and evil, but abstract indignation did not come naturally to me at the age of twenty.

It was, on the whole, a very difficult war to get *into*, and I nearly gave it up altogether after several unsuccessful attempts. The Wrens wouldn't have me on account of my French ancestors, as only the purest of English blood may run through the royal blue veins of the Senior Service. When I reminded the bossy Wren who turned me down about *1066 And All That*, she answered stiffly, 'I am not here to listen to your nonsense, my girl,' and that was that.

The ATS, who accepted me as a volunteer for the Intelligence Corps, took so long to draft me that I gave up waiting, and offered my services to the Foreign Office instead. A spy, I said, was what I wanted to be. The Major who conducted the interview looked me up and down incredulously.

'What on earth do you want to do a thing like that for?' he asked with unnecessary snoot.

'To go and rescue my nanny,' was what I really wanted to howl. 'We left her behind in France, and she loathes the Germans with all her guts.' It would have been interesting to see his face if I *had* said that, but instead I answered soberly, 'I can speak French so you wouldn't notice, and I know the west coast and the South of France pretty well.'

'Really? Well, my girl, that's all very commendable, but I'm afraid it's not enough. Thanks for coming all the same.'

He must have seen my face drop. Indeed, I had quite a job not to burst into tears.

'You really want to get into this war, do you?' he asked more kindly.

'Yes, I do,' was all I could manage to say.

'Go to Cambridge then, and see these people.' And he gave me an address which he scribbled on the back of an empty Players packet. 'These people' turned out to be a white-haired old lady who was doing her bit for the war.

'What can you do?' she asked without looking up, and I delivered my rigmarole once more. She looked up.

'Ah. I suppose you wouldn't go overseas?'

'Of course,' I said. 'Anywhere you like.'

'They are asking for a French-speaking librarian in Algiers. You'd better go and see General Staff Intelligence at the Foreign Office.'

So back to the FO once more, this time armed with a more official-looking bit of paper than the empty cigarette carton. The lady who interviewed me this time looked like a don. She regarded me doubtfully: 'You are very young.

[3]

We don't usually send girls overseas under the age of twenty-four.' What was so mystic, I wondered, about twenty-four?

'Why not?' I asked, kicking myself for not lying about my age, as John had done.

'Well, it's, er ... pretty rough, you know.'

ROUGH! What could be more blissful? I had visions of pitching tents in the desert, tethering camels, fighting my way through clouds of locusts, and everywhere Foreign Legion officers dashing about on white chargers. Nothing in the world would suit me better.

As it turned out, the Foreign Legion did indeed swarm in the streets of Algiers, and romantic-looking Spahis galloped about on their nimble little Arab steeds, with scarlet cloaks flying behind in the wind, *and* locusts crawled into bed with you, and got crunched up in your typewriter. But I never came within sniffing distance of a tent. There was no canvas for girls. That was a privilege reserved entirely for men.

'However,' continued the don lady, 'you look steady enough. Not the flighty type.'

'Oh no,' I said regretfully, 'I'm afraid I've got no talent for *that*.' (And how I envied those who had!)

'Don't be sorry. I wouldn't send you if you had.' And with these words she gave me a staggering number of clothing coupons, and vague instructions about getting *sensible* hot-weather clothes, and to ring her up when I had done my packing and was ready to leave.

But before all this came to pass, my family and I had to make good our escape from France under the very noses of German tanks, bombers and U-boats.

2

THE WORST PART of the great débâcle in France, when
the Germans came thundering over the countryside in
their thousands, was, as far as I was concerned, that we
had left our old nanny Marie behind. Although a Swiss
German herself, or perhaps because of it, she loathed 'les
Boches' as she called them, and would make no bones
about it. I knew she would seek out trouble, and get herself
sent off to some ghastly internment camp in the wilds of
her hated Germany. It was not long, in fact, before she
found an excuse for bashing a German soldier with her
umbrella, and if the friends with whom we left her hadn't
smuggled her out to their château in the country, she
would certainly have been in serious trouble.

But we only learnt about this after the war, so I had four
long years in which to worry about her. I never saw her
again, but when I was stationed in Vienna in 1945, she
wrote in answer to one of my letters, 'How good of you to
remember me. Perhaps I was too hard on you sometimes,
but I hope we may meet again and be happy together.
M. Votre Père had a very bad time in Singapore, but the
Germans were no better here. They stole everything
out of your house, and turned out my wardrobe and my

trunk, and burnt everything in the garden. They even burnt the photograph of my husband and my little baby …' Those were the photographs which had hung on our nursery walls in Venice, and before which we had knelt and prayed and wept on the anniversary of the baby's death.

We reached Bordeaux the morning after it was bombed. The mayor, fearing further unwelcome attentions from the Luftwaffe, promptly declared it an open city. Through the litter of ploughed-up streets and smoking ruins, my mother led us to Great-Aunt Annie Adet's flat. The sister of my paternal grandmother, she still dressed in the Edwardian style, with high lace collars and a black velvet band around her strangled waistline.

Not surprisingly, it was with noticeable lack of enthusiasm that she greeted our scruffy and bemused party. Her flat, having escaped both explosive and incendiary bombs, was impeccable. Her opulent comfort, deriving from the popularity of Cognac Adet on the French market, gave a feeling of indestructible security. The furniture displayed the restrained and elegant well-being of the provincial nobility from which her family descended. I could see that her haughty demeanour, as she came to the door, would not go down very well with Mamma, who, not in the least bit impressed by this grande dame act, said truculently, 'I'm sorry to have to trouble you, but we are refugees, and need shelter for a day or two, until we can get away from this town.'

'Very well, I suppose you'd better come in,' said Aunt Adet with distinct lack of warmth, as she surveyed our dishevelled appearance, rucksacks and all. 'But I hope it won't be for long, and the children had better eat in the kitchen. I can't have crumbs all over my Aubusson in the dining-room.' As this referred to Anne and myself, aged respectively fifteen and eighteen, we felt rather peeved by the remark. But my mother having gratefully accepted the

[6]

conditions of her hospitality, she thawed a little, and we were finally allowed to eat in the conservatory, among the orchids and the exotic ferns.

After our feast of stewed plums (no other food was available by then, as the hordes pouring in from the North had cleaned the place out like locusts), we trooped off to the English Consulate for advice and help. But we were too late. The Consul and his family had departed, leaving several hundred Britons without assistance.

'Go to Bayonne,' counselled the distracted policeman on the doorstep of the Consulate. 'You may find your man there.' So in one body, we all rushed to the station, where total chaos prevailed. Fifth columnists, darting through the crowd, were assiduously spreading panic. 'The enemy are entering the town, the Boche are shooting all British civilians on sight,' and so on, following the well-laid plans of the German propaganda machine.

The heat was annihilating, and with the broiling sun beating down on the glass roof of the station, half-demented children lost in the crowd and shrieking with terror, people fainting with exhaustion and lack of food, it had all the elements of a first-class nightmare.

When the train finally pulled in, there was a stampede, with people climbing through the windows, into the guard's van, onto the driver's plate and balancing on the couplings between the carriages. The porters, running down the platform, were wrenching suitcases out of people's hands and flinging them far out of reach on to other lines. No luggage was allowed on the train, but our rucksacks, the very same which we had used on mountain climbs ever since we were old enough to scrabble up a hill, got by unnoticed.

Bayonne is a delightful town, and in spite of the heat wave and the multitudes thronging the streets, camping on doorsteps and asleep on the pavement, and the total lack of food, I have kept very agreeable memories of it.

[7]

Loudspeakers attached to the plane trees lining the streets announced that the Germans were now in Bordeaux, and that an advance Panzer Division was on its way to the Spanish frontier. Any stray Britons still hanging around were to find their way immediately to St Jean de Luz, where an English boat was at anchor, scheduled to sail at midnight. Trams were leaving for St Jean every half-hour, and into one of these we gratefully piled. The harbour was at a surprisingly short distance, and there, to our overwhelming relief, was the British Army at last, in charge of evacuation operations. And oh, the joy of seeing calm, clean, tidy, cheerful English soldiers at last!

Our British passports worked like magic, and the corporal controlling the entrance to the embarkation quay waved us through with a flourish. There were several hundred stranded English people there already, in quiet orderly groups, and surrounded by hopeful piles of luggage. And not a sign of panic or confusion anywhere in spite of the nagging fear of enemy aircraft. Surreptitiously, we peered at the sky towards the North, dreading the black crosses which had come swooping over the long columns of refugees snaking down the roads of France in the last two months. We were sitting ducks, herded together on the quay, and if they came they would make short shrift of us. About a mile out at sea, our boat lay at anchor, and shuttling back and forth, half a dozen fishing boats were taking the refugees out in loads of about twenty at a time. As darkness fell, the soldiers came clumping through the groups, hissing in hoarse whispers, 'No more talking, please. From now on we mustn't hear another word. The harbour is full of U-boats, and they can hear you *breathing*, so keep your traps shut.'

A thin refreshing drizzle began to fall, and the water was growing choppy. When our turn finally came, poor Christine, my eight-year-old sister, was wilting pitifully, and as we chugged out to sea and the boat bounced higher

[8]

on the churning waves, she gradually turned pea-green, and when she set up a wail of distress, a pullover was promptly stuffed into her mouth. As we reached the ship, the sea was running so high that it was almost impossible to get the fishing boat close enough alongside for the passengers to jump onto the gangway. Over and over again, an enormous wave would lift us wide of the side, just as someone was about to jump over. We were all dreading Christine's turn. As she flatly refused to budge, a sailor grabbed her round the waist, and leapt over the gap with her under his arm, protesting vociferously. No U-boat could have failed to register her indignation, had one been around. But we happened to be lucky.

Finally, and blissfully, we were all on board. It was like waking up after a long and very bad dream. And while the ship was gathering up her skirts and generally preparing to sail, and Anne and I were hanging over the rail, not wanting to miss anything, I remember the shock of seeing several loaves of English bread, all sodden and disintegrating, floating about in the bilge. Starving as we were, it seemed the most insane and wicked waste in the world. To this day I find it difficult to throw away an old crust, even in France, where bread dries up overnight fit to splinter your teeth.

As we climbed on board, the wife of the Consul was sitting, cool and elegant, on some high bit of the boat, swinging her bare brown legs and watching the exhausted rabble piling in helter-skelter. Heavy steel coffers which looked like ammunition boxes were hauled up on deck, and the sailors said these were King Zog of Albania's gold reserves, and at the time, as I goggled at the dazzling golden-haired young queen, only a year older than myself, I little thought that thirty years later I would be presented to her at a London dinner party, under very different circumstances.

My mother disappeared at once with Christine. I believe

that they were sharing a cabin with several other women and children. Anne and I went off in search of sustenance at once. Two thousand Polish troops, who were going to carry on the fight wherever they could, huddled on deck surrounded by their packs, rifles, hand grenades and tin mugs. Climbing over them, we carried out a meticulous inspection, finally settling down on the sailors' sleeping deck, with a large mug of hot sweet tea each, and an enormous lump of bread and margarine. No feast could have tasted better. Gradually more women joined us, herded below by the sailors, until it became evident that they were making their quarters over to us for the rest of the trip. Our guardian angels, as we came to regard them, set up trestle tables for us, and above them they hung rows of hammocks so close to the ceiling that you had to climb onto the table before you could hoist yourself into bed. The whole arrangement, when bulging with female behinds, looked like an enormous swarm of white ants bunched up together and glued to the ceiling.

We slept most of that first day at sea, and towards the evening, half a dozen sailors came clattering in with pails of milky, sugared tea, which we took a little time to get used to, as we had never been allowed sugar in tea or coffee at home. Bad for the teeth. The sea was now quite rough, and although the boat, broad and blunt-nosed, rode the water like a sitting hen, the contents of the tea buckets splashed and slopped around, and from time to time, a whole mug of boiling liquid shot into somebody's lap. Longing for a little light relief, Anne and I greeted these incidents with squeaks of mirth, which went down very badly with the ladies. Several of them, too exhausted to get up, stayed in their hammocks, swinging above our heads as we sat at the tables below. It was appallingly hot and stuffy, as all the portholes had to stay closed because of the blackout.

As soon as we could, we both escaped up on deck, where

we were surprised to see how angry the Atlantic had become. Edged all round the horizon, and blending so well with the general wet greyness of the sea as to be hardly visible, the destroyers of our convoy were speeding along inside the cocoon of their own individual smoke screens. But so far away that, had we been hit, we would have sunk beyond recall long before they had a chance to fish us out. And now that one of our childhood wishes, that coveted shipwreck, was a possibility at last, the prospect was no longer so attractive.

Not that there was much time to think about it. Except for Anne and myself and a few others, most of the women were now so ill that they remained in their hammocks altogether. The sailors had thoughtfully placed empty buckets for their benefit at regular intervals along the tables, and copious use was made of these as we sat at the tables, drinking our sweet tea and munching our bully beef sandwiches. In answer to their cries of distress, Anne and I ran from one to the other with towels, cups of tea or glasses of water, and as this service continued all round the clock throughout the ten long days of our voyage, we got very little sleep. Some of our patients seemed to be rather ill, but our friends the sailors, whom we approached for advice, said that nobody had ever died of sea-sickness.

One of the few other survivors categorically refused to help with our nursing activities, on the grounds that all those gruesome buckets which had to be emptied made her feel quite queasy. A huge creature, with a massive head like a rhino, she sat smothered in several layers of bright tartan rugs, making up her face all day long and moaning incessantly about her ruined holiday and the gross unfairness of life in general. By now the scene on deck was not much more cheerful either. The poor Poles, fresh from their landlocked steppes, and finding themselves at sea for the first time in their lives, were no better off than our women. Everywhere, prostrate khaki forms lay huddled under horse blankets, with only their boots sticking out. It was like a battlefield. What would happen to all those inert shapes if we were torpedoed? 'We'll carry the little dears into the boats in our arms, just don't you worry about them,' said the sailors, whose optimism and cheerfulness were unassailable.

Having by now lost total interest in our destination, we remained unmoved when the news trickled through that we were landing at Southampton.

After all the upheavals of the last few weeks, the greatest surprise as we trudged along the neat, tidy English streets looking for lodgings, were the posters everywhere advertising Saturday night dancing in the Town Hall. Nobody seemed even aware of the chaos, of the thousands of homeless, starving, wounded people, the total collapse of ordinary life and the complete moral disintegration of armies and civilians which reigned barely twenty miles away across the Channel. It was like landing on another planet. The June sun blazed on this lovely afternoon, millions of miles away from the agony and death throes of the Continent. Cheerfulness and good humour bubbled everywhere, and the shops were bulging with food. It was all very strange and wonderful.

Years later, after the war was over, I met the captain of our ship, who told me sadly that HMS *Ettrick* had been torpedoed and sunk in the Atlantic, after long and gallant service on convoy duty. We had apparently been incredibly lucky during our crossing, as U-boats had followed us all the way to England like a pack of sharks.

At the beginning of the war my brother John had been evacuated to Ilfracombe with the cramming establishment at which he was preparing for his exams. Thither we repaired, and my mother dumped us in a local boarding house while she went off prospecting. The glorious summer weather continued, with clear blue skies and the broiling sun. Except for one tiny cove, all the beaches of the Devon coast were mined and bristling with tank traps, gun turrets and enormous rolls of barbed wire. Together with a couple of girls from our boarding house, we went to that little beach every day, swimming and lying in the sun, while I brooded and planned how to get back to France. I knew it was quite hopeless, but all the day-dreaming and wishful thinking helped to tide over the period of readjustment. We were suspended in a kind of limbo, unconsciously gathering our depleted forces for whatever was to come next. Christine, who had till now woken up every night with fearful screams of terror, was beginning to calm down again.

Suddenly one day without warning, and following her wont, my mother reappeared out of the blue. 'Pack your bags,' she ordered. 'We're going to stay with your aunt in Bedford.' So off we went once more.

My aunt's house, a vast abode with long dark corridors, already sheltered nine people, including our twin cousins' nanny, but excluding any other living-in staff. Without hesitation, my uncle offered us all hospitality. His wife, who had always had an easy life in Malaya, with all the houseboys she needed, had buckled down cheerfully to cooking, housework and all the horrors of a wartime household full of young people, and only daily maids to help. Catering was to become increasingly difficult, and for the next few years England was to survive mostly on powdered egg, potatoes and cabbage. Whale meat, which appeared later on fishmonger slabs, never really caught on. A smear of butter and jam, and a small quantity of beef or mutton gristle was obtainable with the ration books every week. Sausages were unrationed, but had to be queued up for, as well as something of unparalleled loathsomeness described as soya links. Owing to Lord Woolton's masterly methods of housekeeping and budgeting on a national scale, there was enough to go round, with a little bit of everything for everybody. You were graded according to your occupation. A bank manager, for instance, got less cheese than an agricultural or a dock worker. Those who existed on one ration book fared worst of all, whereas a baker's dozen like our household, through some principle of compound interest which eludes my understanding, did rather better.

When John, having successfully taken his exams, arrived in Bedford for the holidays, my mother gathered us all in her room and announced her plans for the future. She was going back to Malaya on the next boat, and wanted us all to go with her. John and I, horrified by this suggestion, announced that we couldn't possibly skip the war and leave England at a time like this, as we were quite old enough to do something useful. To our surprise, she made no protest, only demanding that we should be suitably employed before her departure, as she didn't want us idly kicking our heels, looking around for mischief. My uncle, when approached, said of course we could stay in his house as long as we wished, and my aunt, on whom I was to become an extra burden for the next six months, added that her home was our home, and there was plenty of room for everybody.

Within ten days we were both fixed up, and Mamma sailed in an enormous convoy bound for the Far East, with Anne and Christine, and whatever peace of mind she could muster. Initiative, independence, unlimited courage and uncomplaining endurance had always been her most shining virtues, and she was to need every one of them in the years to come.

John, without asking anybody, had enlisted in the Youth Regiment of the Beds and Herts. I answered an advertisement in the local paper for a junior assistant at the County Library, and was summoned for an interview, to which I went with dry throat and quaking knees. Herded with the other seemingly unconcerned applicants, I waited for my turn to appear before the Selection Board. At the end of a long office, the entire senior staff faced me as I advanced uncertainly towards them. The afternoon sun, slanting through the window, glinted on their spectacles, and there wasn't a naked eye between them. Later, when they all became dear friends, I wondered how they could have managed to look so forbidding.

With pounding heart and ears buzzing with fright, I did my best to answer their questions. Which exams had I passed, and what about my school career? (Horrors!) What were my favourite subjects, and above all what books did I read, and which kind of novels did I prefer? Saying regretfully that I didn't care much for novels, but was prepared to read some if necessary, I thought that was the end of that when they dismissed me, saying I was to send the next candidate up to them.

It came as a great surprise to all of us when I heard I had landed the job. For the first year I was to get eleven pounds a month, and this would go up by one pound a year until further notice. The Town Library was a large imposing building near the Corn Exchange, whereas we were housed in Harpur Street in a barnlike construction without central heating, and only two coke fires in the workrooms downstairs. Catering exclusively for the county, we supplied a fresh lot of books to the outlying villages every few weeks. An enormous van, fitted with shelves, was packed to the brim every Friday, and off we went on our rounds, each equipped with a bundle of sand-wiches. The Deputy Chief, Geoffrey Clark, drove the van, with Za, the Senior Assistant, sitting beside him, while the juniors were packed higgledy-piggledy into the back among the bookshelves and with no view at all of the end-less fields of purple cabbage with which the county of Bed-fordshire is closely carpeted.

Unloading the van was a tricky operation. To begin

with, books are fiendish objects to deal with in any number. First of all in cold weather they turn into slabs of ice, numbing the fingers, and when carried about in enormous piles running up the length of the arm way up above the head, obstructing the view, they wrench shoulder muscles apart, and at the least provocation, fold up in the middle, bursting outwards and scattering far and wide, preferably into any puddle within range. Sorting them out again to fit the alphabetical list is a simple job for novels, but non-fiction, being arranged in code, is quite another matter.

In an effort to avoid mishaps, minutely synchronised timing had to be observed. The outgoing books made place for the incoming lot, and the two assistants, loaded up to the eyebrows and with visibility impaired, had somehow or other to avoid a headlong crash, *and* to make sure of using the correct shelf. A moment of inattention could result in hours of searching for one book among several thousand on the van, as we serviced a dozen or more villages in one day. On lovely hot summer days this was delightful, and we had jolly bucolic picnics under haystacks and hedgerows, among the wild flowers of the fields, and the butterflies and the humming bees, so you would forget there was a war on, and we were as happy as schoolchildren on a spree.

Za and Geoffrey were great individualists, both with strong notions of their own. Because of his lack of confidence in the virtue of cows, Geoffrey always had little screw-top jars filled with goat's milk. Za consumed a couple of minute sausage rolls every Friday, and absolutely nothing else. Their views differing in almost every way, they argued a great deal and we listened, voraciously gobbling our marmite sandwiches, and anything else we could sink our teeth into. In the autumn there were blackberries to pick, and mushrooms in the grass, but when the snow lay thick on the ground, or the north wind drove slanting, icy needles of rain along, soaking the books, it was bitingly, hideously cold. Sometimes our boss took pity on us feeble girls, and led us into a café for restoring cups of tea and a quick warm-through before facing the northern blasts again.

Soon after my arrival a new junior joined our ranks, and gravitated to the pasting bench, where I reigned with an enormous brush and a gallon pot of glue. Tania, having just left school with all kinds of glowing honours, was putting in time before embarking on her undergraduate's career at Cambridge. At that time, if you were bright enough you went to university at sixteen or seventeen under a special wartime dispensation.

Together we tore old labels out of the books, and pasted in new ones. With her natural bouncing vigour, Tania threw herself wholeheartedly into the job, finding an endless source of amusement in her near (or far) misses with the glue brush. Her sense of humour was constantly tickled by the hilarity of everyday situations. She would dissolve into breathless mirth at the most anodyne joke, and such incidents as dropping a pile of books on your toes, or sticking a label into the wrong end, would practically induce a seizure. In our bustling, subdued little community, each one of us beavering away at his own job in silence, Tania, quite uninhibited by our reticence, bashed on regardless, serenely unmindful of other people's hang-ups or shyness. Even our newest junior, Daphne, who hardly ever opened her mouth, seemed to liven up a little under the Tania treatment. As an only child, and gregarious in the extreme, she adopted us all as her family, and has remained a firm friend ever since.

After a few weeks' training at the paste bench, I was promoted to shelving. The books returning to the library had to be restored to their rightful places on the shelves in the Stack Room, a kind of icy warehouse full of shelves rising way out of reach. A light, narrow stepladder was provided

[17]

for soaring to the distant heights, and on this I soon learnt to stalk around as if on stilts, from one bookcase to another. Working in the Stack Room, where your breath came out in little puffs of steam, was an ordeal in cold weather. For the first time in my life I got chilblains, and my hands became twisted with angry-looking red lumps, normally dormant, but which stirred at the roots in a torment of itches at the slightest hint of warmth.

Fire-watching, one of Tania's special treats, meant sleeping on the premises, which we took in turns, two at a time. I strongly suspect that when she and I were on duty together, one or two alerts may have passed unnoticed by the time we had laughed ourselves into unconscious exhaustion over our efforts at cooking supper over a gas-ring, one holding the pan while the other stirred the coagulated rubbery lumps reeking of sulphur, which we concocted out of powdered egg and water. Fortunately the great bombing fleets which roared overhead most nights on their way to the Midlands and the industrial North, ignored our unimportant town, except when chased away with some of their load still on board, which they then dropped here and there on the way home. The only occasion on which a few incendiary bombs landed through the roof of the Stack Room, Mr Box, our incomparable caretaker who was on duty that night, dealt with the trouble single-handed without disturbing anybody.

Our Chief, who resided in the large office upstairs where I had been interviewed, actually lived and breathed and had his being in the Middle Ages. Often, as I passed him on the stairs, he glanced up at the clock, sighing gustily, 'Ah, would that we could put the clock back to *those* days!' A born bachelor, who would probably remain one to the end of his days, his gentleness and kindness to us girls was constant and unfailing, considering that we were there on sufferance, *faute de mieux*. Only since the war, and the total disappearance of male assistants, was the awful decision of employing *girls* reluctantly reached. At all times, he and his deputy were most long-suffering with us, although we couldn't carry half as many books as the boys, or haul up single-handed the fully loaded lift, which was operated by ropes unaided by any balancing weight.

In Chaucer Road three more evacuees had joined the household, and that enormous house, already bursting at the seams, stretched still further to accommodate them. And my aunt continued to shop, cook, wash and iron for this army of young people. Yet she still found time to go out and visit her friends, and to hold vast bridge parties at home until the early hours of the morning. The noise in the house was indescribable. My cousins, those wild and intrepid ones who had needed a male nanny in Malaya, as no amah could be found tough enough to control them, were as high-spirited as ever. Louis, the eldest, who had once, when he was eight years old, and to my great delight, placed a fried egg on my head, saying it was my Sunday hat, now enjoyed knocking books out of my hands with a well-aimed cushion. Jean, the next one down the line, crooned at the top of her voice in competition with the sound of the Light Programme which blared out of the various radio sets dotted about the house. Bill was still at school but came home every night, when he took part in the general rumbustiousness, and Jacqueline, the little in-between, who at the age of eight neither fitted in with the teenagers, nor the infant twins, had to lift up her voice loud and long to get any attention at all in the general pande-monium.

Soon after my arrival at the library, Maisie, the 'senior Junior', pink and white of complexion and light-gold of hair, and altogether reliable and conscientious beyond her years, was promoted to take charge of the Branch Library in Dunstable, and we lost an irreplaceable member of staff at Headquarters. After Tania had left for Cambridge, new juniors came and went, but one of those who stuck was

Daphne, the Quiet One. Silent as a mouse she flitted about, and though chubby and well padded, was as light on her feet as thistledown.

It was not long after her departure that Maisie had so improved the service of the Dunstable Branch and enlarged her readership, that she needed an assistant. I asked if I could go, and hooked the job. Maisie found me digs in a little road nestling at the foot of the Downs, with identical houses all in a row, and neat little pinafore gardens in front. My landlady was a spruce Beatrix Potter character with a pussycat face, and her best friend who lived next door, who looked like her twin sister, was so houseproud that her husband was forbidden to cut his nails in the house. Once a week I used to watch him build a tiny bonfire in his back garden, and neatly cut his fingernails into it. That was known as being 'very particler', and was greatly admired.

My landlady's own obsession was electric light. Nobody was allowed to switch it on until after dark and the black-out drill had gone into action. Her husband had a quaint, coy little trick of turning it off at the main as soon as I had got into my weekly bath. My habit of reading in my bedroom was regarded as outrageously extravagant, so that an extra charge was added to my rent for the single light bulb and electric fire in my room, stretching my monthly eleven pounds to its very limit.

Lunch, for the last few days of the month, had to consist of marmite sandwiches, while supper in the parlour of my digs, consumed under the close scrutiny of my hosts, consisted of two slices of bread and margarine (butter on Sundays), one slice of cold bacon, one cold boiled potato and tea, all of which left vast gaping corners, so that I always went hungry to bed.

For the first two or three weeks of each month, when Maisie and I were still in funds, we lunched at the Noah's Ark, the best inn in town, where we had a delicious three-course meal, with unusually good coffee, for two and six-pence a go. Dunstable being a market town, cattle were driven into the square every Thursday to be sold below the Noah's Ark windows, where the farmers, strengthened by their sustaining visits to the Saracen's Head opposite, conducted the proceedings with vigour and a good deal of fruity language, while the unhappy beasts bellowed and roared in protest and indignation. It was a lively, noisy, odorous scene, which added considerable interest to the landscape. Maisie, as a farmer's daughter, brought a pro-fessional eye to bear on it all, and I just enjoyed the fuss and the bustle and all the excitement of the market place.

Gwen and Leah, who were friends of Za's, ran the Ark between them. Gwen, who was an artist, did all the deli-cious cooking, and Leah, an ex-journalist, coped with the accounts and the general management of the establish-ment.

The happy day came when one of their rooms fell vacant and was offered to me for a pound a week. Overjoyed at my luck, I came galloping over to take up the offer. Vacant was indeed the word. Apart from two divan beds, the room was bare. With another pound I acquired three chairs, a table and a stool from the local junk shop. From then on my budget became very much easier to balance. The window sill was my larder and kitchen cupboard combined, which was fine during daylight hours, but became after blackout a complicated performance, parti-cularly when Tania was in charge of the operation.

A large plywood board had to be slotted into the win-dow frame, and as blackout regulations demanded an exact fit, you had to make sure of getting it *the right way up* first go, or it would get stuck in the window, giving rise to every possible kind of trouble. The worst part being that no light could be switched on to aid the proceedings until the fiendish contraption was in place. As I turned off the light, Tania groped, puffing and panting for the hooks. A squeal would inevitably follow as she caught her fingers in the works. And finally a resounding crash announced the collapse of the whole arrangement, pinning Tania to the floor. Bouncing forward to her assistance, I crashed headlong into the wreckage, while she heaved about underneath, weak and choking with mirth. By the time I finally retrieved the sausages and frying pan from the window sill, and order was restored, and we had gobbled our supper, the time was usually getting on for midnight.

The library, directly opposite the police station, was a vast village hall type of structure with large windows, each one of which had to be elaborately blacked out every evening before the light could be switched on. A huge stove which consumed enormous quantities of coke was our most precious luxury and comfort during the two very cold winters I spent there. The stall wherein we both worked, with its two counters for incoming and outgoing traffic, was in the centre between the two doors, each a funnel for the icy draughts.

Saturday was the busiest day of the week, when the whole town queued up at our doors to change their books. Little gangs of schoolchildren trotted in with their sticky tomes, which if not glued together with jam, you could be sure had not been read. I once found a half-chewed kipper used as a bookmark in a *Just William* story, and another time a grimy comb. There was one particular family of half a dozen scruffy little urchins who arrived in a pack, one half carrying the other, all indescribably dirty and with a permanent cold. Maisie took it in her stride when, at the beginning of the winter the eldest of the tribe announced proudly, 'We've been sewn in for the winter today, miss.'

'You mean for the *whole* winter?' I asked incredulously.

'Oh yes, miss. We won't be cut out again until Easter. Me mother sewed me and I sewed them,' she said proudly, pointing at her handiwork on her brothers and sisters.

At about four o'clock, when it was growing dark, Our

Tramp shambled in and settled down comfortably in an armchair by the stove in the middle of the room. First he took off his boots, then made a great to-do of clawing out the sodden layers of newspaper with which they were lined. As he pushed this into the stove, huge waves of thick acrid smoke puffed out and curled around the room. The boots, which were then placed close to the fire to dry, very soon began to emit a special aroma of their own. People turned and stared unbelievingly as he snored, slumped in his chair, while his filthy bare toes twitched and jerked in time with his dreams.

Maisie's patience was endless. Somebody would come in saying, 'This book's no good, dear. Can't see the print. Now the one you gave me last week was lovely. Can you give me another what's the same, you know, with plenty of love and a happy ending?'

'I should think so,' Maisie would reply. 'Can you remember who it was by?'

'Oh don't ask me, love, Somebody Something or Other, *you* know.'

'Well, what was the book called? Do you remember that?'

'No idea, love. Just find me somethink similar, there's a dear, I 'aven't got all day to stand 'ere jawing with you.' And off would go patient Maisie, to the love-story shelves, with her customer waddling after her on swollen ankles and tortured feet.

'I think you're a saint,' I would say at the end of one of those days, when all the matrons of the town had come up with the same request. 'They make me want to scream. I can't imagine how you manage to be so patient.'

'They're tired,' Maisie would reply. 'They work all day, get their children off to school, go charring, do part-time jobs in a factory, and though they're worried sick about their men in the Forces, they are always cheerful. Our job is to help them to keep going. Love stories are their only pleasure.' At which I felt thoroughly ashamed of myself, and tried to emulate her tone and manner for the next half-hour, until my own impatient and arrogant self got the better of me again, and crossness and bad temper returned to take over from the bout of unnatural affability. Dear, kind, sweet, infinitely good Maisie. Sometimes, in a spasm of rebelliousness, I would say to her, 'But you encourage them in their ignorance, to stick in their mud forever. They will never get out of their morass.'

'Can you see,' Maisie would ask with a twinkle, 'Mrs Potter reading Virginia Woolf?' At which of course I collapsed with giggles on the spot. Mrs Potter was one of our favourite matrons, who brought us treats on her baking days, in the shape of little twists of pastry with a cherry on top, or a dollop of her precious jam ration. She had a voluminous bosom which she heaved on to the counter to ease its weight off her short little legs. Her nose was pinched and tinged with blue at the tip, which Maisie said was the sign of a heart condition. Mrs Potter would probably be carried away by her heart in the end. Always speaking in whispers and leaning far over the counter, she would confide the latest news of her pride and joy, her only son, whose name of course, was Sonny. We went through his departure for the Air Force, then for Canada where he was going to train for the Fleet Air Arm, and eventually his return to the UK.

'And now,' said Maisie, who was all-wise and all-understanding, and who could see into the future, 'we must prepare for the final tragedy. Sonny will be shot down, and we will have to comfort Mrs Potter, or at least try to do our best.'

It came even sooner than we feared. One Saturday afternoon Mrs Potter came up in the book queue, and her pinched nose, apart from the blue tip, was red, and so were her eyes. 'It's happened,' Maisie said in a hoarse whisper, 'Sonny's been shot down.'

'I've had the telegram, dears,' said Mrs P., her eyes brimming with tears. 'Sonny. Reported missing.' It was utterly heartbreaking. For once I was first to dash out and search for the story with the big print like the last one, with plenty of love and a happy ending. Beside these two human beings, and with a flash of insight, I suddenly saw myself as odiously selfish, second-rate and shoddy. What was known in my family in the thirties as 'Made in Japan', a term which would certainly no longer apply nowadays.

Out of all the hundreds of people who came to borrow books every week, it would have been very disturbing if we hadn't had any admirers at all. It was Maisie who came off best on that score. One of her beaux, who had a stunning pair of mustachios turning up at the ends, came in every day for a long time, but too bashful to remain in the same room with his beloved, he scuttled straight into the Reference Library, where he presumably suffered agonies of unrequited love. Then one fine day, pressed beyond endurance, he finally plucked up the courage to ask her to elope with him. Kind but firm, Maisie dealt with the situation on the spot, and that was the last we ever saw of the poor lover. Another, of whom we both approved far more, was a good-looking young man who conducted his wooing with musical evenings in the High Street on Thursdays. But these, alas, were ruined for him as Maisie, in the kindness of her heart, always insisted on my sharing the treat as well, thus cruelly thwarting his object, and wrecking his evening.

During the two years I was in Dunstable, all I could collect was one spotty youth who plagued my life for several weeks. He would borrow technical books on nuclear physics, and then as I stamped the date inside, he lisped, leaning far over the counter, 'I am going on the Downs for the day on Sunday, and I would like you to come with me.' The blatant assumption that I would of course love to go was infuriating. Every time I made some polite excuse, until one day he positively hissed, 'I do believe you're making excuses. You don't want to come at all.'

'Well, since you mention it, no I don't'—making it, as I thought, quite final. But the next day an older version of himself turned up at the desk and summoned me to the Reference Library. 'My brother tells me that you are being wilful and difficult. You have no business to behave like that. The boy is serious-minded and wants to get to know you. It's your duty to give him a chance. We Jews have to stick together.'

I gasped, as the light crashed in with a blinding flash. 'Good God,' I exclaimed, 'it's a misunderstanding. I am not Jewish. Your brother has made a mistake. I *am* sorry.' He was furious. 'You led him on,' he shouted. 'You let him believe you were one of us. It's your fault.' And he thumped the table. This was too much. Leaving him to fume by himself, I swept out, banging the door. And that was the end of my spotted swain, and of romance in Dunstable as far as I was concerned.

Gradually a small group of people, anxious to keep up or improve their French, gathered around me. Hearing of my activities the police, not wanting to be left out, asked to join our ranks. The sessions were held in my bedroom at the Noah's Ark, and members were requested to bring their own cushion on which to sit, and one cup apiece for my special home-made blend of Earl Grey and Brooke Bond, with which I regaled them at the end of the class, and which was known as the French girl's cup of hay.

We read Molière's *Bourgeois Gentilhomme*, each one taking a part, after which they had to give me their version of the text. These were lively meetings with everybody chipping in, improving on each other's efforts, and progressing steadily, except for one young constable who, feeling it was all a little above his head, begged for private lessons. He was going to join the army, and when the invasion of France finally came he wanted to be able to chat up the girls in their own language about the flowers of the fields and the birds and the bees. So, bored but patient, I ploughed on with this enterprising youth throughout the cold and snowy winter.

On the tenth of December 1941, Singapore fell. Japanese troops, modelling their methods on the tactics of soldier ants, had been wriggling almost unnoticed down the Peninsula, murdering our soldiers in their tents while fast asleep, dropping on top of them out of trees in daytime, and as soon as the terrain permitted, unfolding their minibicycles and pedalling furiously, silently and relentlessly towards the Equator. Once more my family were fleeing before the invader, this time not from Panzer Divisions, but from an army on two wheels.

In Singapore my father was patrolling the streets with the Home Guard, organised by planters wielding any weapons they could lay their hands on, shotguns, revolvers, Javanese krisses and Malay swords, while the bombardment of the town went on day and night. A troopship in the harbour was loading women and children for a destination unknown, so that there was no other way but to split up. Leaving my father behind, and under unremitting, stupefying aerial bombardment, my mother and the two girls boarded the ship. Advance Japanese parties were already flooding into Singapore, swarming into the British Military Hospital, where they bayoneted the wounded in their beds, while in the streets the valiant Home Guard was being rounded up and clapped into jail. Papa found himself hustled into a minute cell with a Chinese murderer and an opium eater in the last stages of decay.

Transferred to Changi, which had been my great-grandfather's flourishing plantation a hundred years before, the prisoners had to survive for three and a half years on a cup of boiled rice a day, with occasionally a few potato leaves thrown in as a special treat. The potatoes, which were grown by the prisoners, went to the guards. From time to time somebody was dragged away and beheaded for owning a wireless set, while the entire company of prisoners was made to stand hatless and motionless in the sun from dawn till nightfall. After each one of these ordeals, several of the younger men went off their heads or died of sunstroke. But in spite of the dirt and the hunger, the brutality and disease and the total lack of drugs and anaesthetics, my father said that the experience was unreal, more like a dream, and not so very unpleasant if you could resign yourself.

We heard nothing of him for eighteen months, after which my mother, who had eventually landed in Australia, got from the Red Cross the only postcard until the end of the war, saying that he was still alive.

But meanwhile in Dunstable, nobody thought of telling me anything. As far as I knew, they could all have been bombed into pulp, or roasted alive in their bungalow, or machine-gunned on the lawn, or blown sky-high in an ambush. There was no way of finding out anything, so that with visions of Oriental tortures always in my mind, I became even more forgetful and absent-minded than ever. One evening while Maisie was at the hairdresser, leaving me to close down for the night, I did the unforgivable. Coping alone with the sticky little children, the love-story seekers, and throwing out the comatose tramp at closing time, I forgot all about the blackout. As there was no air-raid, no harm was done, but the police station opposite could not possibly close its eyes to all those blazing windows. The next day a very embarrassed young constable presented me with a summons to go before the Magistrate. 'This won't make any difference to our lessons, I hope?' he asked apprehensively.

'That all depends on what the Magistrate will do,' I re
plied.

And when this gentleman fined me two pounds out of
my monthly pittance, I most unfairly informed the poor
young constable, who had nothing whatever to do with
it, that his bees and his flowers had come to an end, and
he would have to join the *Bourgeois Gentilhomme* again if
he wanted to continue with his French lessons.

But throughout this unhappy time the greatest support,
discreet but unfailing, from my friends at Headquarters,
kept me going. On the day of Singapore's final collapse,
and to take my mind off things, Za took me to the ballet
in London, to which treat Geoffrey contributed ten shil-
lings, a sum which went a long way in those days. The
Chief most generously offered to pay my blackout fine for
me, which infinitely kind offer I couldn't possibly accept.
But gestures such as these, and the intention behind them,
are never forgotten.

From time to time, when I had managed to save the fare,
I jumped onto the London train, to sniff the air and pay
a visit to the War Artists' Exhibition. Over the last couple
of years, Tania and I had been keeping an eye on the progress of the contributors. Henry Moore, we thought,
would make a name for himself. After my first encounter
with his Shelter series, I wrote to Tania, 'He grows on you.
He seems to me original and very powerful,' for which
Mr Moore would feel duly gratified, I am sure, if he ever
read these lines. Graham Sutherland, John Piper, Paul
Nash and Anthony Gross were also promoted to future
laurels.

All day I nosed around, picking my way through the
pathetic rubble of tumbled bedrooms, gaping fireplaces,
pulverised furniture, among which the surviving owners
poked about without much hope of rescuing any of their
treasures. Sometimes, after a heavy raid, whole streets
were blocked off altogether, and Graham Sutherland's

Twisted Girders, grotesque lonely lift-shafts, rose above the surrounding ruins in steel loops and whorls, writhing in an inferno of flame against a blood-red sky. Firemen, balancing like tiny insects at the end of their long swaying ladders, hopefully aimed at the raging furnace thin jets of water which instantly fizzled away into clouds of hissing steam.

Around Piccadilly, sitting in doorways or sprawling at the feet of Eros, lounged hundreds of GIs forever chewing the cud, watching the world go by. The chewing-gum industry in those days must have reached an all-time high. Whenever I felt like putting my feet up, I dived underground to one of my numerous ports of call. Many of the attendants of the West End Ladies were my friends, and there I would get a cup of tea thrown in with the penny, and hear the latest about their sons in the Forces, as well as highly coloured accounts and graphic details of Jerry's activities the night before. After which, restored and refreshed, I sallied forth again to explore some more. Sometimes Za came with me and sometimes Tania, but more often than not I was on my own.

At night I repaired to Bloomsbury, to a little hotel patronised by Za, so that there again I had friends. The nights were racked by heavy raids and furious anti-aircraft gunfire, punctuated by the shrilling bells of ambulances and fire engines tearing around the streets of London in a continual stream. After one of these raids I wrote to Tania, 'We had three air-raids last night. The bombs were simply raining all round. Some of them so near that I was bounced out of bed twice.' And on one of those occasions my bed was literally lifted off the floor, and I remember, while climbing back into it, a feeling of mild surprise that the ceiling hadn't come down on top of me. All over the hotel people were probably thinking and doing the same thing. The wise ones had staked a claim in the Underground stations, where jolly parties were in progress every night, with everybody singing the ditty of the moment to the accompaniment of the squeeze-box or the mouth organ. Beds, sleeping bags and double-decker cots, which remained there all through the blitz, lined the platforms, and people in their night-gear quite happily climbed into bed in full view of the passengers catching the last train home. A great many lewd jokes and allusions whipped back and forth, and it was all very matey. But apart from that, very few ever thought of seeking cover by then. Personally I never even saw the inside of an air-raid shelter during the three wartime years I spent in England. Like most people, I far preferred the prospect of being blown up in bed than that of being buried alive in a cellar.

My efforts at war work were haphazard and rather disorganised. It was perhaps just as well that the air-raid siren happened to be perched on the roof outside my bedroom window, as nothing short of its ear-splitting shrieks, which practically punctured the eardrum, would have woken me up. Leaping out of bed, I would scramble into my Civil Defence uniform and race down to the Ambulance Station where I was doing my bit for the war. I remember one particularly freezing night with the moon at its whitest and brightest, and snow inches deep and crisp underfoot, the clocktower of the Town Hall etched against the pale moonlit sky like a black and white fairytale woodcut, while overhead roared the wolf pack of Heinkels and Dorniers on their way to the kill. All round the skyline in the distance anti-aircraft gunfire thudded away hopefully. Dunstable, which must have been one of the safest spots in the land, lay in the path of the great Northern raiders on their way to flatten the Midlands, and night after night the huge enemy fleet thundered overhead, ignoring our unimportant presence below. But on one occasion I excitedly wrote to Tania, 'The post office was bombed last night. Very thrilling.'

Then there were First-Aid nights, when a large and very

energetic housewife let us into some of the secrets of bandaging, and gave us quick sniffs of mustard, phosgene and other gases, which we were from then on expected to identify at the first whiff. The Services Canteen in the High Street also had to be manned, and Mrs Watson the doctor's wife, who was in charge of this particular headache, arranged the shifts, on which appeared and disappeared in turn the entire female population of the town. But in spite of the vast fleet of helpers, nobody ever wanted to wash up. This was before the days of detergents, and I usually found myself paddling in two inches of water in the tiny cupboard used as a kitchen, splashing about in an enamel bowl of tepid water and soda. From time to time I had to cope with the vagaries of the tea-urn, an antique from the Crimean War, full of treacherous little tricks, shooting out lethal jets of steam in unexpected directions. Finally the brute blew up and caught fire, spreading alarm and despondency and causing some nasty burns.

As the weather was beginning to wag its tail after the long grim winter, and I had a week's holiday to be fitted in somewhere, I decided to set off on a walking tour by myself. Just to be tripping along an empty road across desolate and lonely mangold and wurzel fields would give an illusion at least of wide open spaces and unlimited freedom. Strapped to the faithful and now threadbare rucksack which had climbed up the Provençal Baous and nipped out of France under the noses of German tanks and fighters, I set out one fine July morning en route for Cambridge. At the village of Sandy, the first stage of my journey, I indulged in a cup of coffee and a sandwich. This all went according to plan, and on leaving the village, a bundle of rags pushing an old pram with a kettle on top of it shambled up to me and said, 'Mind if I walk along of you, me dear, seeing as how we're both on our own?'

'Not a bit,' I answered affably. 'How far are you going?'

'All the way up to John o' Groats, and then back again.'

'Gosh, that's a long way. What are you doing that for?'

'I've got nothin' else to do, see, I'm on the road like. I used to walk with an old man for a few years, but he kicked the bucket last winter, and now I'm on me own.'

'How sad for you,' I said sympathetically; 'you must be very lonely.'

'Not a bit of it, a regular old so and so he was, at me 'ammer and tongs all the time, and he made me push his bleedin' pack on account of his back.'

'His back? What was the matter with his back?'

'Plumbago. That's what they said at the 'orspital. But he wouldn't have no treatment, not he, and so *I* had to suffer, and push his perishin' pack.'

'Too bad,' I murmured, not knowing what else to say.

'Na, don't you worry yer head about *'im*. Good riddance to bad rubbish. Just put yer pack on me pram, love, and we can take it in turns to push, like. Yer go first, here you are.'

Grabbing the handle, and shoving along the surprisingly heavy 'perishing pack' on its squeaking wheels, I couldn't help wondering what Marie would say if she could see me now, trundling a tramp's pram through the countryside on a fine summer's day.

A few miles on, after a bend in the road, an old barn suddenly appeared, at the sight of which my companion cheered up a good deal.

'Several of me friends ought to be here today, love. It's a grand meeting place and all. Some of them come up all the way from London. Good spot this. Three good walls and a pump. Everythink you need, as you might say. You can kip down with us for the night if you like, sweetheart.' Thanking her politely, I said I would probably push on, though I might stop for a brew-up with them first. Three members of the fraternity had already arrived. Bert was introduced to me as Mr Erbert Potter who come up from

London that morning, and young Sid, new to the life and not very bright in the head, who travelled with his mentor, Mr Fred Webster. Clad in filthy, stinking rags tied together with string, they introduced themselves with grave dignity, and we solemnly sat round in the grass in a circle. Bert lit a fire between two bricks, and my friend took her kettle to fill at the pump. Fred fished out a little screw of tea leaves, and that greatest of all comforters, a cup of tea, was produced. All I had to offer was a packet of glucose tablets, upon which they fell with joyful greed, while I felt modestly gratified to be able to contribute even in a small way to this roadside feast.

'Open yer bag, dearie, and let's see if you've got any-think as could be useful to us, like,' ordered my friend. With a sinking heart I unpacked my rucksack, spreading the contents on the grass for their inspection: a comb, a toothbrush and a tube of toothpaste (with a swift and fervent prayer that they wouldn't pounce on *that*), a small box of water colours, a sketchpad, a paperback edition of Rupert Brooke's poems (I was crazy about him at the time, his looks I suppose, as much as anything else), a magnifying glass and a spare pair of gym shoes size $3\frac{1}{2}$. They stared at my treasures in disgust. 'Na,' said my friend, 'nothing that's no good to nobody there. Pack it up, love, just a load of old rubbish.'

As I said goodbye, she produced a four-leaf clover, saying, 'That's for luck, love; we can all do with a bit of luck, even the queer ones like you.'

Leaving them to their festivities like a bunch of old ghouls around their fire, I got back to the road. A few miles on, a small hamlet stood at a crossroads. As all signs had been done away with at the beginning of the war to foil invaders, it was impossible to guess my direction. Looking around in bewilderment, I wished to goodness I had an internal compass like Marie's, which always told her the exact position of the Southern Cross, from which she had no trouble at all in working out the precise spot on which she stood.

Giving it up as a bad job, and squatting by the roadside, I spread out my Ordnance Survey map to try and make some sense of the situation. In half a second all was clear, and I set off with a firm and confident step. But not for long. Within minutes, a jeep drew up beside me with an officer at the wheel and a policeman beside him.

'I'll have to see your identity card, miss, and I'll be wanting to know what you're up to, walking along the road all by yourself like this,' said the policeman in rich official tones.

'I'm just going to Cambridge for a holiday. No harm in that, is there?'

'Girls don't walk about on their own like that. Looks fishy to me.' The Army officer now spoke up. 'I saw you sitting on the kerb at the crossroads reading your map. Several German parachutists have landed around here recently. We have to be careful, you know.' Hooting with laughter, I swung my rucksack on the verge.

'Well, of course, I've got a sub-machine gun in here, and several hand grenades as well. You'd better have a look for yourselves.' The policeman went down on his knees, and once more my modest possessions were lined up on the grass.

'Looks all right to me, sir,' said the Law. 'I think we can let the young lady go on her way.'

'Okay, hop in, Constable. I'll drive you back.' And swinging the jeep round he sped back towards the hamlet, while I was left to repack my bag once more. That's the end of that, I thought as I watched a cock pheasant waddle busily across the road and a great cloud of rooks squawking around some tall elm trees. Trudging along and feeling at peace with the world, the blissful illusion of unlimited freedom returned, almost as fresh as before, and what I took to be my soul swelled, overflowed and stretched to the far confines of the distant turnip fields. But again not for long. A scream of brakes, and the dreaded jeep was beside me once more. My heart sank out of sight.

'I've come back to give you a lift to Cambridge, if that's where you *really* want to go,' said the officer. 'Jump in and give me your bag.' And he stretched out a helpful hand.

'No thank you!' I said, horrified. 'But thanks most awfully all the same. I want to *walk* there. That's the whole *point*, don't you see? Surely there's nothing odd in that.' He stared at me as if I were quite mad. 'Sounds loopy to me, I must say, but please yourself.' And with a shrug he roared off down the road and out of sight.

By six o'clock, feeling done in, I decided to call it a day, and knocked at the kitchen door of a farmhouse behind a small hedge. This time, remembering my resemblance to a German parachutist in disguise, I said I was a student on a walking tour looking for a bed for the night in exchange for any job that was going. The farmer's wife looked at me doubtfully, then stepped aside. 'All right, come in, and you can help my son paint the scullery. But I expect you would like a cup of tea before you start.' As I was drinking this nectar, a blotchy youth appeared, with damp mousy hair glued to his forehead. 'This is my son Alf,' said the proud parent. Alph, I thought, delighted, Alph, Where the Sacred River Ran, what a romantic name. And the blotches, and the damp hair receded into the background. Alph, on leave from the RAF, was very fed up at having to paint the scullery. Handing me the wire brush, he said, 'Here you are, your turn now while I have a bit of a rest.' The sound of the wire bristles scraping the wall made my flesh creep and my teeth curl, but I carried on stoically while he sat on the kitchen table watching me work through a haze of Woodbine smoke.

'When you done your bit, what you say we go to the flicks tonight?' he asked.

'No thank you. I'm going to bed early if I've got to paint the whole of this room tomorrow. It doesn't look as if *you*'re going to help much.'

'You're a rum one, you are; here, give us the brush,' he said, sliding off the table. 'I'll have a go, and you mix the paint.' He scraped, surrounded by a cloud of dust and smoke, while dry scabs flew off in all directions, and I splashed the paint on until it was too dark to see. With double summer time, it was past eleven when we finally stopped. Our supper, left under a cloth on the table, was the usual slice of cold bacon and cold boiled potatoes, and great wedges of bread and margarine. Alf made some tea and we gobbled our feast hungrily, after which I washed up the cups and plates.

'Goodnight, Alf,' I said. 'We must get the job done good and early tomorrow, as I want to be on my way. See you in the morning.'

'Okay, lass, mind the fleas don't bite.' (I thought it only too likely that they would.)

The sofa I was to sleep on in the parlour looked big enough for a child of twelve. I tried it this way and that, but fell off every time I turned over. Just as I was deciding to sleep on the floor, the door opened and a torch shone on my face. 'You'll never sleep on that thing,' said Alf. 'Come and cuddle up with me.'

'Get out,' I squeaked. 'I'll scream if you come in, and *then* what will your mother say?'

'Oh la dee dah, her ladyship's too good for the farmer's son.'

'Don't be an ass, just buzz off, that's all.'

'Hark at her, buzz orf, buzz orf. Okay, have it your own way.' And he disappeared with his torch.

It took the whole of the next day to finish the job as Alf, no longer anything to do with the romantic Sacred River now, was sulky and uncommunicative, only picking up his brush when he heard his mother's footsteps approaching. By six o'clock, it was done at last. I slapped my brush into the sink and said, good and firm, 'Now I'm O RFF. You will have to clear up.' He was irrepressible. 'Okay, then I'll run you into Cambridge on the back of my motorbike, and we can see a film together.'

'Look,' I said wearily, 'I told you I was on a walking tour. And that doesn't include bike rides.'

Thanking my hostess for her hospitality, I plunged straight into a stubble field across the road. An early crop of oats had already been harvested, and my gym shoes were hardly up to coping with the rigid prickly stalks sticking up all over the field like a bed of nails. Nevertheless I persisted across the unfriendly acres until at last, like the girl in the fairy tale, I came to a cottage door.

My knock brought a buxom housewife to the doorstep. Her head was done up in a turban, her ample bosom taut and well contained, and her rolled-up sleeves revealed shrimp-coloured arms, shiny and clean, with the kind of cleanness which comes from kneading dough. Her serene blue eyes regarded me without surprise. To her I was neither a suspect, a parachutist, a rum one, nor even fishy, but just someone who looked as if she needed a cup of tea. *Dear* Mrs Roberts, I would do *anything* she asked, I thought effusively, as I delivered my rigmarole.

Evacuated from Manchester, she had taken over the cottage and its helpless and fluttery owner, and it seemed, most of the neighbouring households as well. It appeared that they all came in to meat tea with her every day. She was one of those immensely competent women to whom lethargic souls are irresistibly drawn for comfort and re-assurance. It was a relief to be able to relax under her command. For her I was determined to do my very best, remaining there for as long as my allotted task would require.

My job turned out to be lighting the copper and doing the household laundry. Never having washed anything in my born days but my stockings and knickers, the task was rather daunting, but I set to with a will. The copper, a vast metal cauldron built into a corner of an outhouse, had to be filled with water, and a fire lit underneath to get a good boil-up. Paper already being scarce by then, I dragged a dustbin into which an old hen had been plucked, and stuffed the feathers under the copper to get a good blaze going. As soon as I put a match to it, up flew the feathers merrily on high. Great clouds of bright, gay little flames flying, floating, spiralling, pirouetting about, lodging in the rafters, settling on my hands, my clothes and my hair. In a wild panic, I raced into the garden yelling for help. 'Fire! Help, Mrs Roberts, the barn is on fire. Come quick!'

Mrs R., a woman of swift reactions, bounced out of the kitchen, picked up the hose and turned it full on me. Gasping and spluttering, I stood still while I was being put out. She then sped to the outhouse and promptly dealt with the trouble there. In a few minutes it was all over. Standing on the lawn and watching her, I was shaking with great sobs of shock, disappointment, and the awful, awful feeling of having let her down. All my fine plans, my ardent desire to help, my fervent wish to be of use had come to this! She would just think I had been thoughtless and careless, instead of just plain stupid, if that was any better, staring out of the window, while the barn was blazing away under my nose. Sob, sob and re-sob. She would never know that I had *really* wanted to help. Sob again.

After tea, a sumptuous affair of which I managed to swallow not a crumb, such a waste, I humbly asked to be allowed to wash up, which being granted, took a lot of doing as there were nine people to tea. But afterwards, when I offered to milk the cow, my offer was firmly turned down.

3

ALTHOUGH I KNEW that the library had to be manned for the time being, and that my job was a useful part of the war effort, I was beginning to feel restless. Whatever Maisie said, I couldn't really reconcile myself simply to provide love stories for deserving housewives. I longed for something more active. The powerful drive of wanderlust was aroused, stirring subconscious memories lurking in my blood of long-ago ancestral pioneering, and continued prolonged sorties into the unknown. Such must be the drive which prompts wild herds forward in search of pastures new when the smell of migration is in the air. And behind everything else was the ferocious longing, which I hardly dared acknowledge, to have a bash at the enemy myself, and a chance to drive my own vengeful nail into his coffin. Women could at last take part in this kind of vindication, and it was intoxicating, not to be denied.

But here I came up against serious divergence of opinion with our Deputy-Chief, who held that our loyalty was due *first* to the library, and secondly to the country. If the truth be told, neither of us was being quite honest, either with himself or with each other. Geoffrey didn't want to lose another junior assistant, even a mere female, and I was longing to get away, to stretch my wings and see new horizons, all of which was piously clothed in mumbo-jumbo about doing my bit for the war and the country. The result was deadlock, and because the young, once convinced, cannot be contained, I of course won. But I don't think that he ever forgave me. Za, although secretly disapproving, was tolerant and sympathetic, and Maisie, dear Maisie, just thought that people must do what they feel they have to. And so I began to volunteer for this and that and the other, until I was finally swept up into the bosom of the Foreign Office.

When, in answer to their instructions to shop for sensible hot weather clothes, I rang up Bush House to say I was ready to leave whenever they liked, I was told to report there at once.

I was to work in PID for the time being, until a seat on a plane could be found for me. PID, or the Political Intelligence Department of the Foreign Office, controlled information and propaganda to the enemy and all occupied countries, through every form of the media available at the time. Secret services such as the famous SOE (Special Operations Executive), and various others of the same ilk, also flourished under its wing.

Arriving in London with my Sensible Hot Weather Clothes, a copy of *War and Peace* in one volume, and a teddy bear presented to me as a parting gift by my twin cousins who had got bored with him, I repaired to Bloomsbury, where I booked a room in my little hotel for an unspecified length of time.

PID was lodged on the eighth floor of Bush House, and could only be reached by lift, on presentation of a special pass. The landing being solidly wired away from the staircase, we were well and truly behind bars, once inside.

One evening, as I was leaving the office, and checking out of the cage, the corporal on duty at the door said I was wanted in Major Walter's office. It was he who had interviewed me when I first arrived at PID. Now he informed me that I was leaving the next day for Algiers, and would I please refrain from breathing a word about it, and report at Norfolk House at five o'clock the next evening.

'Good luck,' he said, adding gallantly, 'I wish I were coming out with you. All the pretty girls seem to be going out to the Med these days.'

I thanked him politely, and he handed me an envelope. 'Take care of this, and produce it if you're nabbed. It's your Certificate of Capture, and it just says that although you are a civilian, you're not a spy (*would that I were!*) and you're not to be shot on sight.'

'Thank you,' I said, rather taken aback. 'Not that they'll take any notice, mind you,' he added airily, 'but it's worth a try, and anyway General Staff Intelligence insist on it.' And with these comforting words, I was dismissed. Within twenty-four hours of my arrival in Algiers, this document was pinched out of my handbag, so *somebody* must have thought it worth having.

Norfolk House, which was the London headquarters of Allied Forces HQ, was the gathering ground for all those who were flying out to North Africa. A couple of years earlier, a Captain Beauclerk, who was eventually to become my husband, had also reported to the same spot with his unit. And there they had been greeted by their US Commanding Officer, Colonel Heseltine, a veteran of the Mexican War and senior in service to General Eisenhower, with a formal little address beginning with the words, 'Well, Gennelmen, I guess you must know who you are, but as far as *I* know, you might as well be some goddam Medical Unit.' The Colonel was well topped-up. And when the gallant little unit finally came to rest in Algiers where he was in charge of the American side, the Colonel, though not always sober, had nevertheless lost none of his cunning. Richard Crossman, then British Head of the Unit, intrigued successfully for his removal.

Short of equipment, we were at the time the poor relations of the Americans, and very much at their mercy. With this powerful ace up his sleeve, the CO departed at the head of the unit's entire transportation fleet, thus bringing all Psychological Warfare Branch work effectively to a standstill. Mr Crossman was forced to eat humble pie, and Colonel Heseltine made a triumphant return at the head of his vehicles, each one of which was jauntily decorated with his nickname 'Hazy', in bold red letters, to make quite sure the salt was well and truly rubbed in the wound.

From the moment we stepped into the precincts of Norfolk House, we were cut off from the rest of mankind, and were forbidden to use the telephone, or communicate in any other way with the outside world. Apart from myself and a colourful-looking character who turned out to be a BBC correspondent, I was the only civilian there. The others were military personnel, either Army or RAF, and nearly all men at that, apart from four WAAF officers.

After a couple of hours, a coach drew up outside and we all piled in, bound for we knew not what destination. This turned out to be Blackbush airfield, an RAF station. Still closely herded together, we were shepherded out onto the airstrip by half a dozen RAF Military Police, who checked us into our waiting Dakota as we climbed on board. The BBC man, who was wearing a battered panama and a pair of boots hanging round his neck like fieldglasses at the races, plonked himself down beside me. His face twitched with nervous ticks, and he wore broad scarlet braces over an electric blue shirt. As far as entertainment value went, he was, alas, a dead loss. A hip flask, which was his constant companion, seemed to fulfil all his needs.

My first time in an aircraft, it turned out to be a baptism of fire. We sat in two rows facing each other along the fuselage, on hard cold tin seats, with mail bags, our various

[43]

bits of luggage, tin hats and khaki nylon parachutes piled on the floor between our feet. The flight to Bristol took a couple of hours, by which time it was quite dark and very cold. Arriving in the middle of an air raid, the sky was ablaze with searchlights, bursts of gunfire, and the heavy black crosses of enemy bombers etched against the flashing lights. Our nimble pilot managed to weave his way through the falling incendiary bombs, and the bright red streams of racing bullets from the ground defences. Great fires were leaping into the sky over Bristol in the distance. As soon as we touched down, we were hustled out of the aircraft, into Nissen huts, while the pilot rushed his 'crate' into its secret hiding hole. A warm and cosy canteen welcomed us all into its bosom, as if everything were perfectly normal, as indeed it was for them, poor souls, since they were bombed almost every night of the year during that period of the war.

After a comforting meal of brown Windsor soup, powdered egg omelette and fried dehydrated potatoes, we felt equal to anything, but it was announced that we would not take off again until the raid was over. I extracted *War and Peace* from my suitcase, and settled down for a good read. From time to time, when a bomb landed rather close, the Nissen hut was practically shaken off its moorings and then good-naturedly settled down again. When the sirens announced the end of the raid, we were told to line up to be weighed with our luggage before embarking once more. And then to my surprise, I heard my name being called out over the loudspeaker, asking me to come to the head of the queue. Lugging my case, and wondering what on earth it was about, I pushed forward to the weighing desk. The corporal in charge said as I gave my name, 'Since you are underweight, do you mind taking these kippers on your luggage allowance?' Beside me stood a portly Brigadier, holding up an enormous bunch of kippers for my inspection.

'I'd be delighted,' I said dubiously, 'but couldn't they be wrapped up?'

'Don't you worry about that, my dear,' said the Brigadier. 'I will look after them myself, so long as we can put them down to you on the list. I'm a bit overweight myself, you see (yes, I could see that). And these kippers just tip the balance.' I stepped on to the scales with my case at my feet, *War and Peace* under one arm and the kippers dangling from the other fist.

'Thanks a lot,' said the portly officer, relieving me of my odoriferous burden. 'I wish I could invite you to breakfast, but I'm going to Cairo, and you're dropping off at Algiers, aren't you?' The situation was saved, and a happy Brigadier climbed into the plane behind me.

Although there were still some pretty big fires burning high into the sky in the direction of Bristol, the cold starlit February night gave out a great feeling of peace and serenity. It was difficult to believe that all that twinkling space had been filled only a couple of hours earlier with roaring death machines. After we had been laboriously gaining height for about half an hour, the co-pilot appeared and announced that, as we had an enemy fighter on our tail, we would have to go up to twelve thousand feet. 'Some of you may be a bit short of wind, but that's nothing to worry about. And I'm afraid it's going to be very cold.'

That was an understatement. Not only was there absolutely no heating in the aircraft, but the porthole behind my head had a nasty twist in its thread, letting in an icy jet of air straight into my left ear. Opening my suitcase, I buried my feet into its contents, and got out a pullover to wrap around my neck. For the next five hours, we sat shivering in stoic silence. Nobody came to tell us when we lost our enemy tail, and perhaps he followed us all the way. The coast of Portugal, along which we flew, was like a scene in Fairyland. By now completely accustomed to the severest blackout as we were, the coastal illuminations below were a surprise and a delight which made us forget our state of near numbness.

An hour later, blessed dawn was breaking over the sea, and life revived a little in our refrigerated hearts. Soon after, we were dropping fast out of the sky and pointing straight at the Rock of Gibraltar. How anyone can ever land on that narrow strip of concrete jutting out into the sea is still a mystery to me. With great skill, the pilot negotiated it successfully, and we were soon standing on the tarmac in the warm scented air, and with all the noise and frantic bustle of a Mediterranean port churning around us. Little dark men scuttled about among our luggage, shouting, pushing, seizing and dropping cases and kitbags, while antiquated taxis dashed about after prospective fares like Dinky toys all over the landing strip. It was all gloriously, delightfully astonishing.

The WAAF officers and I were corralled into a high-domed taxi of Edwardian design by one of the little brown men who didn't trouble to ask for directions. Taking the bit between his teeth, he plunged into the crowd, banging furiously on his door to forge himself a way through. Hooting was forbidden in Gibraltar in those days, though why I can't imagine, as they were making just as much noise, all of them shouting and yelling and banging on their doors as they went. A couple of troop carriers having landed just before us, the airfield was milling with people. Our driver, almost frantic with frustration, bellowed and drummed on his door to such effect that it suddenly jumped off its hinges and dropped to the ground. In the back we all gasped with dismay. 'Never mind,' he shouted. 'Never mind, now we go,' and with that he hurled his vehicle into a gap in the crowd. We screeched our way round the hairpin bends to the Rock Hotel. Everything which had, it seemed, been prearranged, was working like magic. Shown upstairs to bedrooms with balconies hanging over the sea far below, we were brought breakfast on rolling tables, and were told we could have a bath and sleep the whole morning, as our plane wasn't taking off again until three in the afternoon. But who wanted to sleep! Revived after a bath and our copious breakfast, we set off up the road to call on the Rock apes. Although not at home that day, they were in residence throughout the war, and still are. If ever they leave, says Tradition, Gibraltar will be lost to the British Crown.

The flight to Algiers that afternoon was calm and uneventful. So far all had gone so well that we assumed this smooth and dreamlike order would continue forever. But the magic carpet which had brought us thus far without a hitch, mysteriously withdrew its powers as it set us down on the shores of Araby. To begin with, the airfield at Maison Blanche had obviously been badly bombed, and as most undamaged spots had already been bagged by other aircraft, ours could hardly find enough space on which to land.

As we stumbled across rough ground, dragging our luggage towards the RAF station in the distance, the Service personnel were being met and wafted away in a firm and orderly fashion. The stragglers, consisting of the BBC man, half a dozen Morse operators and myself, in other words the PWB contingent, were left to our own devices. Since none of them appeared to know what to do, besides hopefully hanging around waiting for something to happen, I decided to set off in search of information. Nobody I came across had ever heard of the Psychological Warfare Branch. Were there any taxis, or coaches, or trams into Algiers? Haha, they said, where did I think I was? Piccadilly Circus? Well, was there a telephone I could use somewhere? No, no, nothing like that, unless the Station Commander allowed me to use his ... Well, it was most irregular, but just for once ...

It took over half an hour to get through to PWB

Headquarters. Never having come across field telephones before, I didn't realise how lucky I was to get through in under half a day. Major Twist, the Chief Administration Officer, eventually came on the line. *Who* had arrived? And what had we come for? Who had sent us? Oh well, since we were there, we might as well get into Algiers and come up and see him. Meanwhile, he would try to sort things out, and discover what it was all about. No, he hadn't been told we were coming, and he certainly didn't need us. In fact there was no job for any of us. He really couldn't imagine why ... How were we to get into Algiers? Oh well, he'd better send a car out to collect us. Yes, we must just wait until he could find one. No, he had no idea how long it would take. We must just wait, that was all, thank you.

When we finally arrived in his office, he said he couldn't make head or tail of all this nonsense. What on earth did London think they were up to, sending out whole gangs of people like that without any warning? By then my patience was ebbing fast. I grabbed the telephone on his desk, and said, 'Don't worry. I'll ring up PID and say there's been a muddle, and we will be back on the next plane.'

Snatching the receiver out of my hand, he growled, 'You'll do no such thing. If anybody rings up London, I do it.'

I sat down and stared at him expectantly. There was a long silence. Finally he said, 'You will all report to Basic News in the morning. They are always screaming for bodies there. Perhaps they can make use of you.'

At this point his secretary, who was to become a great friend, and who had been winking at me for some time, piped up. 'I will take you to the Mess now and get you signed on. Follow me.' In the Mess, a large requisitioned hotel on the hill, we were quickly allocated bedrooms, and told that dinner started at six o'clock, American fashion.

The secretary, whose name was Maria, came up to my room with me. 'You may not think so now, but you will love it here,' she said comfortingly.

'Yes,' I said with great conviction, 'I know I will like it. But will I be able to do what they expect of me? I thought I was coming out here to be a librarian.' Maria laughed. 'My dear, there is no library in PWB. Just put that out of your head.'

'That's what I'm worried about,' I said. 'You see, that's all I can do. Books, and library work.'

'Well, lucky you,' she laughed. 'You will be quite unique. There will be no competition.' And she left me to go and change for dinner.

The bedroom, which was quite small, contained a double bed, a wardrobe and two minute bedside tables. A small balcony looked down into the street five floors below, and a bathroom en suite completed my kingdom. What more could anybody want? Maria had said that the cleaning was done by Italian prisoners of war. Hum.

Fluffing out my feathers with a great effort, I went down to dinner at six-thirty. The dining-room, already full of people a good deal older than myself, formed a gallery above the large entrance hall. Feeling like a snail without a shell, I sat down at a bench at one of the tables, next to a gentle-looking, grey-haired girl.

'You're new here, aren't you?' she asked. It was just like being back at school!

'Just arrived from England today,' I answered.

'Oh well, you'll soon get used to it. Don't drink the tap water and don't walk about barefoot, or you'll get worms under your toenails. We don't have bread here. Instead we get these dog biscuits. Okay if you have good teeth, and they are said to be stuffed with vitamins. Who are you sharing with?'

'Sharing what?'

'Your bed of course.'

'My *bed*? I didn't know I was sharing it with anyone!'

'Oh yes, you must be. We are all two to a bed,' she assured me calmly.

It was quite correct. When I climbed into the double bed that night I was on my own, but when I awoke in the morning, there was another head on the pillow beside me. A curious sensation. While it was still fast asleep, I crept out to the balcony to watch the sun rise over the warships in the bay below.

Captain Borden, with his high sloping forehead and receding chin, had an alert, birdlike look, and as Major Twist's Adjutant, he conducted the administration of the Unit. Calm and cheerful, he was never ruffled, and made up by friendly helpfulness for all his superior officer's funny little ways.

'Come and see me at my office,' he told me when I came down to breakfast that first morning. 'I'll sort you out and put you in the picture.'

Psychological Warfare Branch, or PWB, as it was called by everybody in the Mediterranean theatre of war, was a vast, loosely strung organisation, part military and part civilian, which controlled the local Press, produced leaflets to be dropped into enemy territory, set up newsrooms known as Prop Shops, with photographs and pamphlets on every possible subject to do with the Allies and their progress in the war. There was also something called D Section, the Intelligence Department, and several other groups of cloak and dagger activity of which we knew very little. Propaganda, which is of course what we were up to, was a dirty word. Political or Psychological Warfare were the only words to be used in connection with our activities. It was some time before I even realised that I was in White, as opposed to Black propaganda.

Ronald Seth described PWB as the Truth Benders in his

book of the same title. But I think this applied solely to the Black Warriors. We never knew exactly what they were up to. From time to time a neighbour at the dinner table, or at a party, would murmur in your ear as someone walked past, 'He's in Black, you know,' and immediately a glowing aura would spread around him. They greatly enjoyed their prestige, and indeed who wouldn't? Some of them were thorough-going Walter Mittys and one handsome, swashbuckling Colonel, whom I got to know quite well, habitually lived in such a world of fantasy that he had to get himself medically readjusted in a psychiatric hospital before he could cope with ordinary life again after the war.

PWB was made up of British and American military personnel as well as civilian linguists, press and advertising writers, art designers, film and radio experts, ex-soldiers from the front whose nerves had been shattered by the horrors of war, and who had special knowledge of occupied territories, or skills of one kind or another. People came and went, from London and Washington and New York and back again, from secret missions 'behind the lines' in the Balkans, from Cairo and our various units strung along the coast. All this, Captain Borden explained patiently. I was to work in the News Department, but what exactly my duties were to consist of would be decided by the Editor.

Basic News, which operated in the News and Information Section, was known as the nerve centre of the Mediterranean Forces. We worked in a vast and bustling room with a long central table heaped high with enormous untidy piles of paper into which everybody dipped, scrabbling around for tips and inspiration. The Editor usually stood in the middle of the floor, half buried in mountains of red-hot war news, reading through the bulletins which came over the teleprinters. It was he who decided which items would be used, and who was to write what. When he came across something which caught his fancy, he tore it off and tossed it over to the writer concerned. 'Here's a bulletin for you, Jo. No, make it a flash.' These news bulletins were continually being cancelled or contradicted, reinstated or added to, then 'killed' once more. Sometimes you had to write a story and tear it up half a dozen times. And occasionally, when it was already being read over the air, you had to persuade the news reader to take back everything he had said. 'Ladies and gentlemen, in the light of new events which have just occurred . . .' the announcer would have to say, and then you made yourself scarce because his wrath when he came out of the studio was something fearful to behold.

To begin with, as a junior, I got all the small, politically insignificant stories, more features than news items. When one of them had to be translated into French for the local Press, this fell to my lot as well. What I really liked best of all was to be sent out to 'cover' a story. Some small happening in the town, the opening of an exhibition, celebrations or murders or funerals, fires, riots, or anything else which might make a paragraph of local events for our morning news sheet and the French papers. These items had to be written twice, in English and in French. All humble 'cub reporter' stuff, but great fun to do, as it gave me a chance to go and explore, and poke my nose into all kinds of corners.

One assignment I shall never forget was inspecting the Kasbah before Bubonic Plague had broken out, and the great summer washdown, when all the fire hoses of the town were turned on at the top, and left to run down the streets for several days, until all the filth had been washed away into the sea.

A French officer who knew the Kasbah like his own pocket accompanied me on this jaunt, as no woman could trust herself alone in that glorious den of thieves, murderers, white-slavers, opium smokers, spies, smugglers and black marketeers of every possible degree. We picked our way through mounds of rotting refuse piled outside every doorway in the narrow streets. Down the centre ran the drain into which all household slops were flung out of doors and windows. The stench, which was overwhelming, seemed to leave the inhabitants unmoved. Everybody was selling something, squatting on his doorstep. Little heaps of rusty old twisted nails, empty cartridge cases, cigarette ends, the odd broken-down boot, and in one place, a row of skinned and bleeding camels' heads with huge staring nightmare eyes, lined up on the cobbles of the street. In the prostitutes' district, which was the least filthy of all the narrow little lanes, the ladies sat at the windows of their tiny houses no bigger than cupboards, and exchanged obscene remarks about us in French as we passed. Some addressed us personally in jeering tones, to which my escort, who wasn't in the least ruffled, answered in kind. After that, to make up for the horrors and the smells, he took me to lunch at the Officers' Club, the Cercle Interallié, where we ate in the paved shady courtyard, beside a little fountain trickling into a mosaic pond filled with water lilies.

My head never stopped spinning during the first few days I spent in Basic News. The noise and the bustle, the constant comings and goings, the numerous telephones all ringing together, the shouting and the swearing and the cursing of the newsmen, the nostalgic crooning of Italian prisoners of war singing O Sole Mio, as they swept enormous mountains of paper from one end of the room to the other, the continual ticking, and the smell and the heat of the teleprinters, were unbearably distracting. Thinking I would never get used to such goings-on, I had, out of sheer self-protection, to learn how to switch off and get on with my work in the general pandemonium.

After a few weeks, I was put in charge of the daily news bulletin which went off to Averell Harriman, the American

Ambassador in Moscow. From the various wire trays lying about on the table, I had to take my pick of what seemed appropriate for this gentleman's instruction, then wind it all into as readable a story as I was able to construct. As long as I minded my own business, I was left very much to my own devices. In Rome the following winter I was put in charge of the same service to our SOE (Special Operations Executive) Unit in the Balkans, that group of heroic and exotic young men who lived at the highest pitch at all times, camping in the mountains with the Partisans, and in constant danger of their lives.

In the midst of all this, new, astonishing experiences were continually springing up all round, and among them, my introduction to the facts of life occurred one hot and sticky night in June. And it was not, alas, the romantic experience you might expect from such a setting.

I was, as so often happened, on night duty in the Newsroom. As the youngest member of our unit, my elders and betters who arranged the schedule, stuck me on the night shift as often as they could decently get away with, thus leaving themselves with nice long evenings in which to enjoy any social life that might be going. As the war, which had moved on to Italy, was mercifully over in North Africa, blackout regulations, unless there was a raid on, no longer applied, and all our windows were wide open onto the balcony. The electric fans churned the air around, expelling the evil fumes of hot teleprinter oil and nicotine, and sucking in the steamy jasmine-laden air from outside. Lined along the walls, the teleprinters ticked and hummed, each one equipped with a GI operator who punched the keys and kicked the works when the machinery broke down, as so often happened.

The night editor, an American newsman from New York, had gone out for a late dinner, promising to bring me back a sandwich and a bottle of Coca Cola, and leaving me in charge of half a dozen GIs, a couple of Arab typists called Dandelion and Sweet Pea, and the news network covering the entire European theatre of war. The communiqués and bulletins trickled in from Tass in Moscow, Associated Press, Reuters, and Ministry of Information in London, the Office of War Information in New York, Psychological Warfare Executive in Cairo, and our own unit in Tunis. On top of that, an endless stream of information from the enemy, picked up on the air at the monitoring base at nearby Bouzarea, came pouring in day and night. All this had to be sorted out, turned from usually unintelligible cablese into English, or rather American, and rapidly typed out by Dandelion and Sweet Pea for distribution to Allied Forces Headquarters, for the edification of our Supreme Commander, General Eisenhower, and his political advisers, Harold Macmillan and Robert Murphy.

Then came the War Correspondents, the leaflet writers, a moody lot which included Richard Llewellyn, Ritchie Calder, Peter Noble, Norman Cameron, ex-Private John Atack (who had to be defrocked by the Army in order to join and mix with us on an equal footing, as we all had officer status), and many others. Their prose, which was dropped behind enemy lines and infiltrated one or two other top-secret destinations, kept them hard at it, concocting convincing arguments to seduce the Italians away from the Axis, and the German soldiers to desert their own lines. The briefest of all leaflets I ever saw, simply stated phonetically, in large black letters, 'EI SÖRRENDER'. Armed with these, the enemy came streaming over no-man's land to give themselves up, when they finally realised that they had lost the war.

As Outgoing News Editor, I had to make sure that none of these organisations, each one in its own eyes more important than the next, was left out. If anything went wrong, I was not, thank God, held ultimately responsible in the eyes of Authority. It was the Editor, whether he was on the job or on the rampage, who would get it in the neck. But he would of course make sure that I got my share of the trouncing. And so I never enjoyed being left on my own for very long, even in the middle of the night, when the war usually simmered down to sporadic engagements here and there on its various fronts.

By midnight Merc (short for Mercury of course), the Editor, had not yet returned. Obviously he was taking a chance with 'that goddamn Limey, no damn good at anything', as he always described me. Nothing more was coming over the teleprinters, which had gone silent, except for an occasional spurt of activity. A drunken message came over from Tunis: 'The bugs are biting Buddy, and Jesus, how they bite.' To which I scribbled back, 'He who lies down with dogs must expect to catch their fleas,' and when the GI had punched this out on his keyboard with an appreciative chortle, I said, 'Come on, boys, let's pack it up for tonight.'

We locked the doors and crowded into the lift, yawning and, as far as I was concerned, longing for bed. In the hall downstairs, a couple of war correspondents bustled in to check on the late news.

'We've closed down for the night,' I informed them. 'Nothing going on at all. Dead as mutton.' And to the GIs, but without much hope, 'Will someone give me a ride home?' It was always advisable, when speaking to them, specially if you wanted a favour, to use their own language. But in spite of that, I drew a blank.

'Not tonight, honey,' answered one of them. 'We're going to the PX for doughnuts and coffee.' This was their Post Exchange, a kind of super canteen and YMCA combined.

'Stick to the middle of the steps and you'll be okay,' advised another.

'Solong, baby, mind the bugs don't bite.' What a hope, I thought gloomily, when the bugs stop biting the heavens will fall, and I crossed the road, extracting my hatpin from my handbag. Unobtrusive but effective, this was my only means of self-defence against drunks, footpads, or just plain ordinary white-slavers. When one of these gentlemen sneaked out of the shadows and made a grab, I plunged the hatpin into his soft parts, which sent him reeling back with howls of pain, while I took to my heels as fast as I could, leaping up the town steps like an antelope. Algiers, built on the side of a hill, is made up of parallel streets one above the other, with enormous flights of stone steps linking the different levels.

The PWB offices were lodged in the Maison d'Agriculture, at sea level, while our Mess, the Hotel Cornouailles, was five streets up the hill. Our lives ding-donged between those two squalid, bug-ridden buildings. Lovely gleaming white Algiers, La Ville Blanche, was at that time a witches' cauldron seething with the scum of Europe, a kind of enormous abscess gathering on the ultimate fringe of the tidal wave of war. The political situation was inextricably confused. Admiral Darlan, Marshal Pétain's heir apparent, who had been visiting his son in Algiers, had been taken prisoner by the Americans when they landed in North Africa. The Germans, infuriated by this move, retaliated by occupying the whole of France. Darlan, disgusted by the new turn of events, sided with the Americans on condition that they made him head of the French régime in North Africa.

Outraged by this volte-face on the part of their Allies, PID in London didn't know which way to turn. Up till that moment, their instructions to Richard Crossman, the Big White Chief of the British Section of PWB Algiers, had been to shoot down Darlan with all the psychological ammunition at his disposal. How could he now turn round and declare Darlan to be his favourite blue-eyed boy?

De Gaulle, who was anyway enraged at not having been told of the landings, attacked Churchill, and one more of those famous explosions between the English Bulldog and the Croix de Lorraine took place. Then suddenly, the situation resolved itself, when a young man marched up to Darlan's office and shot him dead. The assassin was promptly dealt with by a French firing squad, and the matter was dropped with great relief by all concerned. But in a place like Algiers, a *scandale* of this magnitude was not going to get by without its quota of rumour. The story went round that the young man had been hired for the deed by the brother of General d'Astier de la Vigerie, who had been secretly despatched to Algiers by de Gaulle, to find out on the spot what was going on. While he was there, and thinking he might as well kill two birds with one stone, the emissary imported the Duc de Guise, heir to the French throne, with the intention of setting him up in Darlan's place. Plots and counter-plots which might well have appealed to Shakespeare.

Political prisoners, numbering up to ten thousand, were rotting in the most appalling conditions in French concentration camps dotted about in the desert. The Communists and the local French Fascists were conducting their own private warfare, and black marketeers of every shade and description did a roaring trade in stolen army equipment, while the local rich amassed more wealth by selling wine, olive oil and farm produce to German agents, who smuggled their loot home by way of Spain. In the streets at night the Arabs killed the Jews, and the Jews killed the Arabs, while the Goums, who walked about hand in hand in their long skirts, with curved scimitars hanging from their belts, knifed anybody who came along for a packet of cigarettes. Muslims, whom I had always understood to be teetotal, lay about in drunken ragged heaps on window sills and spread out on the town steps, so you had to leap over their prostrate forms on your way to work in the morning.

So on the whole, and what with one thing and another, lingering in the streets at night was inadvisable, and my main wish was to get back to the Mess as quickly as possible. Not that *that* was so very much safer either. The night before, while we were at dinner, tucking into our spam and dog biscuits, a gang of Arabs had smashed the plate glass of the front door and crashed into the hall of the hotel with blood-curdling war cries, and a week earlier a servant had been found murdered for no apparent reason in the Hotel Regina, the War Correspondents' Mess.

'Any messages?' I asked the corporal on night duty at the Cornouailles when I got in.

'Plenty of them, honey, but not for you.' So, the lift being out of order as usual, I toiled up the five floors to my bedroom.

Miriam, my bed-mate, was standing on the balcony stark naked, etched in black against the enormous white disc of the moon. There was no other light in the room, as our only electric bulb had presumably been borrowed by a neighbour, or nicked by the Italian prisoner of war who cleaned us out (in more ways than one) to sell on the black market. Turning to face me, Miriam rolled her huge breasts, almost as large as the moon, and stared in silence. And I wondered, for a split second, if what they said about her in the Mess could be true—that she was moonstruck, and went a bit funny in the head at the time of the full moon. On the bed, choking and spluttering through his snores, lay an equally unclothed man. I recognised the flat back of his head as belonging to an American lieutenant from the herd of young stallions who habitually followed Miriam around. Absolutely fascinated, I stared at one then the other in hypnotised silence. She came back into the room. 'Am I disturbing you?' I asked inanely, not knowing what else to say.

'Not in the least,' came the reply. 'But we don't want you in here, ducky. Get into the bathroom and stay there until I call you.'

Resignedly, I picked up *War and Peace* from the dressing

table, and shut the bathroom door after me. The tiny dark blue bulb, obviously a hangover from blackout days, gave out only a faint glimmer of light, making it difficult to see the print. Perching myself on the loo as the only available seat, I tried to concentrate on the Retreat from Moscow. Soon the bed beyond the door began to creak and groan. Knocks, bumps and high-pitched wails reached my ears. All very puzzling. I couldn't *think* what they were at.

The late hour and the effort of trying to decipher the almost invisible print made me feel very drowsy. As I was thinking of lying down on the dirty linoleum floor, a faint grating and scraping behind the bath announced that the cockroaches were on the move. They were advancing in a body for their midnight feast, as I always saved up crumbs from our breakfast dog biscuits for their benefit. These I now laid out for my friends in a heart-shaped pattern on the floor. Cockroaches are more brainy than most people give them credit for, and if you take a little trouble, you can teach them some simple tricks. My roaches now arranged themselves in an artistic pattern around their crumbs, instead of rushing about in all directions as ants undoubtedly would have done. First of all cockroaches are not beetles, but close cousins of the stick insect, and secondly they are not dirty, as their detractors would have you believe. Only the adult cocks, curiously enough, grow wings, the hens presumably finding them an unnecessary encumbrance. Be that as it may, their presence was a comfort to me that night.

Suddenly there was a fearful crash on the other side of the door, followed by a muffled moan. Oh God, I thought, there goes our bed. Curse and triple curse that girl. And then, as I was beginning to feel sorry for myself, the Voice of Common Sense stirred in the dark. 'That's Life. If you don't like it go home, but don't snivel.' And I opened the bathroom door to assess the damage. The bed, thank goodness, was still on its feet, but the Loot (our affectionate pet name for Lootenant, as the Americans called them) was lying face down on the floor. Miriam, sprawling across the double bed, was fast asleep. Picking up Don Juan by the ankles, I dragged him out to the corridor, then thoughtfully stuffed his clothes under his head. So these are the Facts of Life, I thought to myself, adding this new item to my growing store of knowledge with appreciative interest.

4

AFTER MY VISIT to the Kasbah, I was not in the least surprised when one fine morning Major Twist stood up in the middle of breakfast and announced that nobody would be allowed out of the Mess until further notice, on account of the Bubonic Plague which had broken out in Algiers. There was a great unseemly cheer from the assembled company. It was like the unexpected announcement of a picnic in a prep school. And needless to say, it started a bout of drinking such as had never been seen before in the Cornouailles Hotel. The dice came out the minute the tables were cleared of breakfast, and poker games were soon in progress. The supply of Scotch having rapidly run dry, gin and Bourbon took its place, and I left them all to stew in their own liquor.

Collecting my painting gear together, I climbed into my bikini and set off for the roof of the hotel. From up there the most staggering view prevailed. Looking north, the whole bay of Algiers was full of warships dotted about on the deep purple of the sea. Hanging my legs over the edge, I peered ten floors down into the street below, where tiny shrouded figures fluttered about like ghosts, spreading clouds of Bubonic bugs around, instead of keeping them cosily tucked up at home in the Kasbah.

While my colleagues were boozing and squabbling over their cards in the steaming heat of the dining-room downstairs, I spent those plague-ridden days roasting, snoozing and painting in glorious solitude in the scorching African sun, all the while serenely breathing in the poisoned air. As far as I remember the disease raged for a couple of weeks only, and no member of our forces contracted it. Nobody seemed to know how many of the poor locals were carried away to the Moslem cemetery on the hill, but the Allies took prompt action, and it never approached medieval proportions.

One day, soon after this, we awoke to a white world ... SNOW? *Impossible*, on the North African coastline, on a hot summer day! Standing on the balcony and looking round, as far as you could see everything was shrouded in this extraordinary white mantle. The palm trees looked incongruous in the little public gardens next door, and the enormous Barbary figs were positively grotesque. The air was full of fine powdery white flakes, wafting gently out of the sky, floating slowly, suspended, light as thistledown, hovering and rocking to and fro. Dressing in a flash, I pelted down the stairs to find out what extraordinary new phenomenon had hit the town. Could it be the End of the World?

The Mess Officer was standing in the hall, staring out of the glass doors. Rushing up to him, I asked what on earth was happening.

'Nobody knows exactly. At AFHQ they think Vesuvius is blowing his top. It seems an awful long way, but if the wind is in our direction, it could be ash from the big bang.'

'All the way from Naples?' I said, goggling. It seemed incredible. 'There must be a pretty awful mess over there ...'

'Not necessarily. It could be mostly this stuff puffing out, instead of a rock eruption. Anyway we'll soon find out. And now, I must get back to work.'

Back to work? It wasn't even eight o'clock. Whatever time did he start? Never, in all the time I was there, did I see him out of humour. As our Gallant Allies would put it, he had the most godawful job in the world, the most troublesome people to deal with, all those tetchy, grousy, gripy, ulcerated newsmen who never got to meals on time, those overstrung leaflet and radio writers, always atwitch with tattered nerves and ragged, disintegrating egos, and incurable drunks who kept the staff up all night, and were then sick on the stairs as they crawled up to bed while everybody was coming down to breakfast. All this, and worse still he took in his stride, dealing with each situation calmly and competently, and with never a word of complaint.

On the whole we all got on pretty well, but early in the morning, when everybody was recovering from the night before, the relations between the Allies tended to be a little on the strained side. 'Where would you goddam bastards be without our Aid?' was frequently heard at breakfast, to be answered with 'And where would *you* be if we hadn't held out alone fighting the war for you for a whole year?' And the exchange of pleasantries would continue until hangovers lifted a little, and the hour of the first pre-prandial Scotch approached. These newsmen were tough cookies with marshmallow hearts. Their rheumy eyes would tinge with unwholesome liquid at the slightest hint of emotion in the air. When their copy wasn't straight news, it oozed with mush and sobstuff.

Chanticleer Leclerc (he had a French grandfather) somehow usually found himself seated opposite me at breakfast at the long central table in the morning, where I wolfed my dried-egg pancake and maple syrup (with the addition of a slice of bacon when a convoy had come in), with one eye on the Basic News sheet, counting the printing errors.

'How you can swallow that stuff beats me,' was his usual greeting. Poor Chant's head was palpitating visibly with the magnitude of his hangover. A waitress dumped a pancake under his nose.

'Christ, take that goddam stuff away,' he roared, 'and bring me some corfee.' The waitress scuttled away with the plate. 'How you doin', honey?' he then asked solicitously.

'I'm doing fine, thanks, Chant.'

'You doin' fine? Gee, that's swell, how am *I* doin', kid?'

'You doin' just fine, Chant,' I answered with my mouth full, trying to reassure him.

'That's right, honey, you doin' fine and I'm doin' fine. Let no one deny it. I'll tear apart anyone who denies it.'

'Don't worry, Chant, everyone knows you're a regular guy.'

'Say!' He thumped the table. 'Did you hear that? She says I'm a regular guy. Did you really mean that, kid?' he suddenly asked suspiciously.

'Sure I meant it, Chant,' I said, hastily swallowing a last mouthful of limp, tepid pancake. He stared at me uncertainly, as a great belch rumbled up his belly, and his elbow slipped off the table, knocking the cup of scalding coffee into his lap.

'Jesus,' he panted, mopping up the mess. 'Sure you don't think I'm stewed?'

'No, Chant, I don't think you're stewed. You're just soaked,' and I beetled down the stairs, rather ashamed of my feeble little pun. It was some time before he shambled into the office, having had to change his trousers first.

'Christ,' he grumbled as he tottered in. 'Why is everybody so goddam tight-assed this morning?'

'Sit down, Chant,' said the Editor. 'I got sumpen special for you today.'

'That's swell, Merc, how you doin', Merc?'

'I'm doin' fine, Chant, here's your copy, Chant. I've

kept it for you. Do it real good, Chant, I'm countin' on you.'

'Sure, boss, just as you say, I'll make it a knockout,' he wheezed, peering at the paper upside down with his lashless little yellow eyes. Settling down at his typewriter he folded his arms on it, laid his head down to rest and snored the morning away undisturbed. He was all washed up.

One evening in Basic News, in the midst of our usual noise, muddle and confusion, a great treat was conferred upon us, and we received a visitation from Marlene Dietrich. Conducted by the American Head of PWB, she willowed into the room on those dazzling million-dollar legs of hers. Dressed in the dark green uniform of the US Women's Army, to which she had added an extra touch by winding round her head and neck a green chiffon scarf whose ends floated seductively behind her back like gossamer seaweed, she tripped around the room asking questions about our stinking, overheating, irascible teleprinters and Morse-code equipment. The newsmen, silenced for once, followed her round with dazed, bemused eyes. In a flash, she was gone, but to my surprise her presence, however brief, had given us all an unexpected lift. This must be the effect, I thought, which all those great film stars' constant tours of the theatres of war must have on the troops they visited ... and about which I had felt pretty cynical until now. Psychological Warfare indeed. I was being caught in the meshes of my own net!

About a week later, a convoy was leaving the harbour en route for Salerno, and there was an air-raid warning, not that you would notice anything special, but AFHQ said so, and we had to close all the windows and drop the blinds and show no chink of light. The heat from the machines was terrible. The only fan in working order had unscrewed itself from the ceiling the day before and become airborne, screaming its way across the room and crashing through the window. Landing in the street

[66]

below, it had been snatched up by an Arab before anyone had time to gallop downstairs to retrieve it. And that was that. Having finished their letters home, the newsmen had packed up and gone back to the Mess. The Night Editor was struggling with yards of yellow telex sheets twined round him like the multiple arms of an octopus, while the Morse operators at the end of the room were having a little celebration of their own with a bottle of Scotch. From time to time the Editor croaked 'Bulletin ... Flash ... Bulletin,' and tearing off a section of the long strip of paper, flung it at me across the central table. It was getting on for midnight, and my copy was nearly finished. Surely he must stop soon. There couldn't be any more engagements at that hour. A few patrols into no-man's land perhaps, but these could appear in tomorrow's news sheet.

'I'm taking my copy to the studio,' I said. 'Furze must have a few minutes to read it before he goes on the air. You know the state he gets into otherwise.'

'Sure, kid, you do that.'

Ripping the sheet out of my typewriter, I gathered up the other pages and tore down the corridor to the studios.

'What the hell are you doing with that script? Why haven't I had it yet? Look at the time, girl. Here, gimme that,' and he grabbed it out of my hand.

The door burst open and the Arab office boy poked his head in, waving a sheet of paper. 'Flash, zur, queek,' he said.

'Godammit!' roared Furze, snatching up the flash. 'It isn't even typed! How the hell does he expect me to read cablese over the air?'

The Night Editor came trotting down the corridor. 'Say, Butch, you got that flash? Make it a lead for the Russian Communiqué.'

'Damn your goddam eyes,' fumed Furze. 'I'm on the air in three minutes' time, and I haven't even read the goddam script. Go to hell.'

[67]

'Take it easy, kid, you're on the air now,' remarked the Editor, pointing at the light. Furze simmered down at once, and his voice became suave: 'Ici la radio des Forces Alliées à Alger. Vous allez entendre les informations en langue française.' His French was faultless, without a trace of accent. The Editor and I stepped quietly out of the cork-lined studio and closed the door. Back in the newsroom, the Arab boy was standing by the desk with a fat grin on his face, and a yellow sheet in his hand. 'Flash, zur,' he said.

'What!' barked the Editor. 'Christ! Kill that flash,' he snapped, hurling the paper at me.

'But it's on the air,' I protested. 'It's too late.'

'KILL THAT FLASH,' he roared. 'Send out a kill.' Almost weeping for Furze, I banged out a kill on the type-writer and raced back to the studios with it.

'How did he take it?' asked the Editor when I returned.

'Dropped down dead,' I said.

'Boloney. Tell him it was only put out by AP to spite Reuters for having gotten in first on the landings.'

I said I was going round to Home's office to listen to the show on his set.

'Sure, kid, go right ahead. I'm going back to the hotel. Close the place down, won't you?'

'Okay, goodnight.'

'So long, baby, I'm playing poker with the Colonel and the other guys. Come and join us when you get back.'

'Grrr ... Thanks awfully,' I said, and bustled off to Home's office, which was in fact a cosy little kitchen. Home was perched on the draining board, fiddling with the knobs of a radio set lodged in the sink and padded with newspaper. The floor was kneedeep in reams of yellow despatches, the last three days' news which he kept around for reference. After that, he poked about among the litter, picked out the meat and stuffed it into the little oven for safe keeping. The rest was borne away in mountains by the Italian prisoners of war who cleaned out the office.

'Come on in and listen to the show,' said Home hospitably. I jumped up on the draining board beside him.

'Furze is upset,' I said.

'Is that so? What's gotten into him?'

'Usual stuff. Script late. Flash at the last minute, then
a kill.'

'Too bad. Swell guy, Furze, but he worries too much.
He'll have an ulcer before he's twenty-five, wait and see.'

Furze's smooth French sentences were filling the room.
He had spent the last two years before the war at the Sor-
bonne, and had certainly made the most of it. Home lit
a couple of Camels and handed one to me. We were great
buddies. As an elderly man of thirty-two, he was high up in
the hierarchy, even senior to the Night Editor. Occasionally he deserted his kitchen and sauntered into Basic
News, where he settled down to a typewriter next to me
at the long table, passing irreverent remarks, just loud
enough to be heard, about our colleagues, and the Editor
in particular. These reduced me to fits of choking giggles
which I tried to turn into hiccups whenever I caught the
Editor's smouldering eye fixed upon us.

Home Parks, dear Home (short for Homer) said I looked
like his wife, which I found immensely flattering, until I
saw her photograph, when I realised that it was just ami-
able waffle to oil the works and promote cordial relations
between the Allies. Mrs Home Parks was a regular Holly-
wood dame with large gleaming domino teeth, toothpick
eyelashes, dramatic hollow cheeks and beautiful black
smooth hair, silky as a labrador's coat.

As I was so often on the night shift, he would from time
to time, to cheer me up, send round little gifts by despatch
rider. And as I hammered away at the typewriter in a cloud
of whirring mosquitoes, with the soggy night steaming
in through the windows, one of these motorbike riders,
all booted and spurred like an astronaut, would come
clattering into the newsroom daintily bearing an orchid

snitched from some scented Arabian garden, or a saucer of Turkish delight filched off a dinner-party table somewhere in Algiers. 'With the compliments of Mr Parks, mam,' boomed the cosmonaut through his echoing helmet, 'and he hopes to come by later if he gets through with his conference in time.' Once in a while, he would turn up to take me out to dinner around seven o'clock. The Editor would bristle with indignation.

'See here, buddy, I know you're a big shot, but she's got to do the midnight communiqué, and she's not going out to no goddam dinner with you or anybody else.'

'Sure she is, and you will just have to do that communiqué yourself, and *your* dame will have to wait tonight. Come along, sugar, my jeep's outside. Let's get going.'

'You can't disrupt my joint like that, you sonofabitch,' growled my boss, as we dived into the lift. I knew retribution would come later, but for the time being it was worth it. We would have a delicious dinner at some expensive black market restaurant, in a little paved courtyard with a splashing fountain and a few stately date-palms all a-twitter with fluttery little birds.

On other occasions, he would collect me after the midnight communiqué, and we would stroll off to a little public garden on the side of the hill where we perched on the town steps in the full light of the moon and well clear of the treacherous shadows, where unfriendly shapes lurked with greed, hatred and God alone knew what other murderous thoughts writhing like snakes in their hearts. From our vantage point, we watched the fishermen's boats swaying gently on the waters of the harbour, and further out at sea, the big destroyers and cruisers tethered to their anchors and gleaming softly in the moonlight. In the dark blue sky above, shooting stars criss-crossed over our heads like fiery knitting needles, and it looked sometimes as if they would come streaking out of heaven and land at our feet, while the palm trees of the square creaked and rustled in their rat-infested sleep.

Home would tell me about his easy leisured life in the Deep South, where the Cake-Walk had originated. And this, he explained, started with the slaves' imitation of their masters' way of walking, which they found excruciatingly comical, while the victims of this derision, ignorant of the true motives, encouraged the slaves in their antics, rewarding a good performance with a slice of cake. He would tell me about the Queen of the United States, his raving beauty of a wife, whom he missed so much, until sooner or later I dropped off, and he clapped his hands and said it was time for me to go to bed. We always parted in the hall of the hotel, and though we all upheld the fiction that he lived there too, everybody knew that he shared a flat somewhere or other with one or other of his conferences. When it was time for me to be posted to Italy, he said, 'That's just grand, baby, gee I sure wish I could be around to keep an eye on you. But you'll be okay, little Limey. Just keep going your own way and don't let nobody nark you.'

'But I don't want to go, Home, I love it here,' I said, feeling very sad.

'When you begin to feel like that about a place, it's time to move on, honey, soldiers don't grow roots.'

I did indeed love Algiers, with all its dazzling whiteness under the burning lapis-lazuli sky, with its gently rustling breezes, its filthy streets and sinister Kasbah, the ferocity of its night life, the proud insolence of its inhabitants who had been in no way intimidated by the thundering armed forces rolling over their land, and above all the astounding white glare of the moon which was my constant companion during my endless spells of night duty.

The great advantage of the night shift was that you had the whole day to yourself to do whatever you pleased. In the scorching heat of high summer, a weapons carrier, which we christened the Madrague Mail, on loan from the British Army, was laid on for the benefit of the night staff. This included the Morse operators, some immensely intellectual Jews who had been rescued from the terrible concentration camps in the desert, and had very soon found refuge in the bear garden of PWB, where they provided a useful contribution to German leaflets and radio, and various other secret operations never discussed by anybody.

There was one jovial little Doctor of Law who looked like Toad of Toad Hall, two gigantic porpoises known as the Ballooning Brothers, one lugubrious-looking Hungarian sergeant, and among the younger set, a Captain from the Jewish Brigade named David, who was as bright and clever and funny as you could wish. Later on, he took a leading part in the repatriation of the Jews to Israel, and under the very nose of the Royal Navy he transported shiploads of immigrants into the Chosen Land.

'Any other Navy would have shot us to pieces,' he told me years later, when I saw him again in Jerusalem. 'When I told them in London what I was preparing to do, they said, "Good luck to you, old boy, let's hope you get through, but we will have to do our job." ' He loved the British and their careless nonchalance, their unflappable, easy-going ways, and would have been very happy living in England. His conscience, however, drove him to settle in Israel, and to take an active part in its government.

Max Wilde, from the Dutch Section of the BBC, and Allsebrook Ross-Williamson, the brother of the playwright, often came too, as well as Elliott, a very Anglicised American sergeant who later became an officer. This motley crew set off every morning after breakfast, piled up in the back of the lorry, which was driven army style by an Other Rank and his mate, bumping and swaying along the coast road all the way to the Madrague. We passed Arab families on the march in war formation. In case of mines, the wives came first, then the children, followed by the donkey, and lastly the lord and master bringing up the rear. A few tents sometimes huddled in the dust, with a camel tethered beside a clump of spiny cactus which he munched pensively, swivelling his jaws from side to side.

It usually took about an hour to reach our destination. This was a small sandy cove, with concrete sea-defences tucked away among the dunes, every one of them containing several families who would creep out and goggle at us, and our lunatic habits, such as lying half naked in the fierce noonday sun, when all sensible beings wrapped themselves up in heavy burnouses and blankets to keep out the heat, and crouched in the shade of tree or tent. A larger concrete hut on stilts served as a primitive kind of officers' Mess, where Other Ranks, in shorts and heavy army boots, clattered about waiting on us at lunch, serving bully beef, raw onion, tinned peaches and sour Algerian wine.

These were glorious lazy days. In Algiers we lived with the war every minute of the day (and night, as far as I was concerned). It was the subject of every conversation, and the bulletins and news sheets were our only reading matter. At the Madrague, the war was light-years away. We nattered on for hours, or rather they talked in French, English or German, whichever came most readily, and I listened. They were earnest, cultured, serious-minded men, and they discussed books, literary magazines, the techniques and interpretations of various conductors, and the culture of pre-war Germany and Central Europe was a subject of never-ending fascination for me. Only when, sooner or later, they embarked on politics, did my pea-brain snap shut with an audible click, and I ran down to the sea and flopped into the tepid, weed-laden water. Finally, stunned with sun and wine, and itching all over with the heavy salt of the sea, we climbed back into the lorry and trundled off to Algiers and one more hot night of work.

[73]

Sometimes, though, I had an evening off; as this seldom followed a set pattern, I never knew the reason for my luck, and forbore to ask questions, in case it was all a mistake. There was always plenty to do. ENSA put on a splendidly spirited show of the *Pirates of Penzance* in army uniform, as all the costumes had been rifled by an Arab gang just before opening night. Much help was forthcoming from the audience, who had several suggestions to make in loud voices in the first act. As the actors tiresomely ignored these thoughtful hints, a small group of spectators climbed onto the stage during the second act to demonstrate their points. When even this was ignored, they gave up in disgust and put on a little rival show of their own in the dress circle, to demonstrate how the *Pirates of Penzance* should really be presented. The local theatre was also very active and quite ambitious in its choice of plays. While I was there, they gave us *L'École des Femmes*, and *Le Malade Imaginaire* of Molière, as well as *Manon Lescaut*.

On Sundays we often went to the races with the War Correspondents outside Algiers. Rupert Downing, who had gone through the great débâcle in France in 1940 and written a book about it, regarded himself as an expert on horse flesh. Before placing our bets, we trooped round to the stables to view the local talent, which he pinched and prodded on the hocks, then, looking the horse in the mouth, he peered at his ageing yellow teeth with a worried frown. Never for a moment doubting his judgment, I still preferred to follow the example of his colleagues, Godfrey Talbot, Eric Linklater and all the rest, who swopped cigarettes with the Arab grooms for accurate information about the winner of the next race. In this manner I always came away a few hundred francs better off at the end of the day.

The first time I went to the Officers' Club, which catered for all the Services, we danced to a first-class RAF band in the steamy hot cellar which had been requisitioned for the purpose. I went on one of my free evenings with Maria, who now shared my bed since Miriam's departure, and Andrew, her fiancé, who had brought along a friend of his to amuse me. Dependable and solid as a brick, they thought I would be safe with him. Alas, nobody wants to dance with a brick, not even one made of solid gold. So when a promising young flight-lieutenant with a fresh face and a lot of rather long fair hair came along and asked me to dance, I jumped up with alacrity under the brick's disapproving nose. We danced around loosely for a few minutes, until he suddenly clutched me to his bosom with a great gusty sigh. As it was much too hot for this kind of dancing, I tried to prise myself loose, but the more I pulled away, the tighter he gripped me with his damp, slippery arms. His khaki shirt and shorts were already dripping with perspiration, and little beads of sweat trickled down his pretty pink boy's face. Locked in a vice, I danced on as best I could, growing more miserably uncomfortable every minute.

'Why don't you relax?' he asked presently. 'You're making very heavy weather of it.'

'Why do you dance with a revolver in your pocket?' I asked peevishly.

'Does it worry you?'

'Well, it's most uncomfortable.' Again I tried to ease away, but he only clasped me tighter. From time to time, one of his legs squeezed in between mine in a most familiar fashion. And all the while the revolver was grinding away.

'Do take it out of your pocket,' I pleaded. 'I promise you it won't get stolen. My friends will look after it for you.' Instead of replying, he began to lick my ear, just like a spaniel.

'For God's sake, what are you up to now?' I snapped irritably.

'I like the salty taste,' he said. Oh dear, I thought, another bomb-happy case. I suppose I must be nice to him. The bomb-happies, as we called them, were the poor ones who, in the official war language, had suffered shell-shock in the front line. Later on, when these pitiful cases multiplied in the blood, sweat, and mud of the Italian campaign, AFHQ installed a psychiatric hospital at Caserta, where these unhappy young men would, it was hoped, be restored to their senses. And so, with anger turning to pity in my heart, I went on dancing, clasped tightly to his chest, and with my behind sticking out like an S-bend, as far away from his wretched revolver as possible.

Directly the music stopped, I raced back to our table, where I found Maria and Andrew doubled up in their chairs, in helpless fits of laughter. Just one more of these situations which other people seemed to find hilarious, and which completely eluded my sense of humour.

My next visit to the Officers' Club was no luckier. This time a Major, who sometimes bumped into me in the hall of my office, and then glared when I apologised, strolled up to our table. He introduced himself to Maria, who agreed that she knew him by sight, and invited him to join us. But he asked me to dance instead.

'I know all about you,' he announced as we began to shuffle around the floor. 'You're the tiddler from Basic News, and a proper greenhorn at that.'

'What on earth is that?' I asked.

'I bet you've never even been kissed,' he added scornfully, without bothering to answer my question.

'Oh yes I have,' I said indignantly. 'At least once.' He roared with laughter as he shoved me roughly around through the dancing couples. I didn't like his tone, and I didn't much care for his manners either.

'You're lucky to have met me,' he announced next. 'You'll know a thing or two by the time I've finished with you.'

'What sort of thing?' I asked nervously.

'Wait and see. It's time you grew up.' He didn't sound

like my sort of chap at all, and I said I wanted to go back and sit down.

'We will sit down when I decide. And I'll pick you up at your hotel tomorrow for lunch. One o'clock sharp and don't be late, or I'll come up to your bedroom to dig you out.'

When we were climbing into our double bed that night, I told Maria that I didn't care for that Major at all, and I wished she hadn't asked him to join us.

'He's a Man of the World, and perfectly all right. Don't worry.' She was obviously impressed by his high-handed manner. 'He thinks you're too shy and need waking up a bit.'

'Ho. And what does Andrew think of him?'

'That he is a very good soldier, and his men would go through fire for him.'

'That may well be, but I am not one of his men, and he is not going to push me around as he pleases.' And privately I reflected that if *I* needed bringing on, *he* could certainly do with a little putting down. Tiddler indeed! What he had yet to find out was that *this* tiddler had teeth, and would bite if pushed too far. But my chance to draw blood didn't present itself for some time to come.

The next day, terrified he should come up to my room, I was in the hall at one o'clock sharp when he marched in to pick me up. An Arab chauffeur drove us out to lunch, mostly on two wheels, so that I was continually hurled against the Major who, totally ignoring my apologies, never opened his mouth the whole way. Perhaps to rattle me, he kept this up throughout the meal so that, in order to bolster my tottering courage and stiffen my twanging nerves, I drank far too much of the local white wine with which he kept refilling my glass. With more experience, I would have avoided the trap. But there has to be a first time for everything.

By now I was bitterly regretting my chums, who would

[77]

be conducting their intellectual conversation over their wine and bully beef on the terrace of the little concrete hut at the Madrague. This Major, I decided, was going to drop out of my life this very day. I had no intention of ever seeing him again.

'Come on, my girl,' he finally deigned to say. 'Drink up your coffee, we must be off.' I couldn't understand why there was so much hurry. It had been a record lunch, throughout which he kept looking at his watch. At two o'clock sharp the car dropped us at the Maison d'Agriculture. He bundled me into the lift, and we got out on the second floor.

'Where on earth are we going?' I asked rather thickly, as the wine was beginning to take effect.

'You'll see. Your education is about to begin.'

My insides tightened and lurched at the sound of this. What on earth was he plotting? 'I want to go back to my hotel,' I said nervously.

Ignoring this, he stopped outside an office door and glued his eye to the keyhole. Then, with a satisfied grunt, he stepped back. Pushing my head down he whispered, 'Take a look at that and tell me what you think.'

Intrigued I obediently put my eye to the keyhole and peered through, staring uncomprehendingly at the scene before me. Unable to make any sense of it, I switched over to the other eye for a second opinion, and suddenly, light crashed in with a loud bang. 'Good God,' I gasped, staggering away from the door. 'It's ... it's ... what dogs do in the streets, isn't it?'

'Shut up, you goose, they'll hear you,' he hissed, clapping his hand over my mouth and propelling me, struggling, towards the lift.

'Why did you make me watch it?' I wailed. 'You're absolutely beastly ... Perfectly horrible ...'

'Don't be such an ass. People love it. You will love it too when you get used to it.' By then we were back in the car.

'I shan't, and I want to go back to the hotel. Take me back at once.'

'Don't be such a ruddy little fool. You've got to grow up sooner or later. Can't you see how they are all shielding you? As long as you stick around with your crowd, you'll never learn a thing.'

'I know as much as I want to,' I said with all the dignity I could muster. 'Please take me back to the hotel at once.'

'You are coming back to my Mess with me. From now on I am taking you in hand, and I will show you what life is about. In no time you will be thanking me for my kindness and trouble.'

'I won't. Take me back at once or I'll jump out of the car.' The one who was loving it was the chauffeur, whose head was screwed round on his neck like an owl's. A great big grin like a slice of melon split his face in half.

'You're not due back till six o'clock, so there's plenty of time. You're coming with me.'

'No I'm not,' I shouted, and opened the car door.

'Sit down,' he ordered, dragging me back. 'I'll hit you if you don't stop struggling.' I kicked him on the shin as hard as I could, and with a growl of pain, he slapped my face, catching me in the eye with his signet ring on the way. I collapsed in a flood of tears.

'You bloody little bitch. All right, go back to your kennel. You'll never be any good, and mind you don't cross my path again.' And he told the driver to return to the Cornouailles.

As I didn't feel up to coping with the eccentricities of the lift, I staggered up the five flights of stairs and dropped on the bed, choking with tears. Flooded with the afternoon sun, the little room was like a furnace. Throbbing with shock and misery, I lay on the burning sheets, with my head threatening to split asunder, and my left eyeball slowly swelling out of its socket.

[79]

After a while I went to the bathroom to be sick, and by six o'clock I felt so ill that no power on earth could have dragged me to the Newsroom. Maria, who returned from her office at that time to change for dinner, said I must have got sunstroke, and had better get into bed and stay there.

All night I tossed from side to side, aching in every limb, shivering like a jelly and hardly able to bear the pain in my head. I couldn't remember feeling so ill since I had pneumonia in Vence ten years before, and was wrapped up in sodden ice-cold sheets to bring down the fever. In the morning Maria took my temperature, and said I must go to hospital at once.

'Oh no,' I groaned, 'Not hospital. If you get me some aspirin I will be quite all right by this evening.'

'I will go and see Major Twist,' she answered, and tripped off to breakfast on her high-heeled sandals. An hour later she telephoned me, saying that a car was at the door of the hotel to take me to hospital, and would I please get my night things together and be off as soon as possible. In a way it was a relief to get out of the tiny bedroom, with its steamy air and dripping walls. Still shivering violently, I packed my washing things, *War and Peace* and my bear, and set off at a perilous wobble down the five flights of stairs. The smells coming up from the kitchen—fried spam, rancid oil and cigarette smoke—made my insides heave, but I managed to get to the car without disaster. The driver was a French colonial who was hiring out his own car to the Occupying Forces. He was kind and full of sympathy.

'It's too bad a young girl like you being away from home and having to go to a rough hospital full of terrible soldiers,' he remarked as we screeched round the first bend. Touched by his concern and aching all over as I was, I still could not really feel sorry for myself. PWB, lunatic though it was, and the Army, working hand in hand, were not really doing a bad job in looking after us. To have a private car sent round to your doorstep to take you to hospital in the midst of the vast and ponderous nonsense of a complicated world war was not a bad effort.

'Well,' I said lamely, 'you know, c'est la guerre.'

But he stuck to his point. 'I wouldn't let *my* daughter go off on her own to a military hospital like that. You're a brave girl. If there's anything I can ever do for you, let me know. I shall be at your service.' This sort of talk does any girl good to hear. With an eye sticking out like a great, glistening, dark-blue Carlsbad plum, and shivering with ague, I was all the more grateful, and my morale went up a couple of notches in consequence. Shaking his head and clucking with disapproval, he put me down on the front step and handed me his card. 'Telephone me when you are better and I will come and pick you up, mademoiselle, and good luck.' Greatly comforted by all this milk of human kindness, I approached the reception desk with less alarm and trepidation than I had expected.

The sister who took my temperature said, 'We will have to put you in isolation until we are sure that you are not infectious.' This suited me down to the ground, and the bare cell they gave me, with a concrete floor and an iron bedstead with an army blanket for sole furniture, was absolutely all I wanted. 'Thank you, Sister, this is perfect,' I said gratefully, and she gave me a sharp look, as if she suspected me of pulling her leg.

'Get into bed as quick as you can, and the MO will come and see you later on. Watch out for the mosquito net.' As she pronounced these words, it came crashing down on top of me.

'Just pull the string and it will go up again. You'll get used to it.'

I sank into a kind of coma, and didn't come round again until an orderly clattered into the room in shorts and army boots, bearing a cup of cocoa. As he handed this to me, the mosquito net came tumbling down, knocking the cup out of my hand.

'Is this some sort of joke?' I asked faintly.

'No, miss, it just happens,' answered the orderly, patiently going down on his knees to retrieve the mug.

'You mean every time?'

'Yes, miss, every time,' he answered in matter-of-fact tones.

'Couldn't we move the bed?'

'Then you wouldn't have the net over your head, and the mosquitoes would get at you.'

'I'm not sure I wouldn't rather have them,' I muttered, 'and please don't bother to bring me another cup. I don't really want it.'

'Oh I never do, miss. One cup is the ration.' And he scrunched out of the room on his bulbous high-shine boots.

Later that evening, the MO came to pay me a visit. As he chummily sat on my bed, the net came down and enveloped him in its folds.

'I see they've put you in the fly-trap,' he remarked as he disentangled himself from the swathes of netting. 'We'll get you out of here as soon as we can. But we will have to see first what the blood test says.'

The blood sample, when duly stewed and curdled, proclaimed that I had malaria. The MO seemed surprised. 'I expect you feel like a good dose of strychnine and be done with it, don't you?' he asked sympathetically. 'And I bet you've been giving the Mepacrine a miss, eh?' These little yellow tablets stood about in saucers on all the dining-room tables in the Mess. Those who took the prescribed daily dose developed custard-coloured eyeballs delicately streaked with a fine network of red veins. Yes, I had been giving the Mepacrine a miss.

My black eye drew very little sympathy from him.

'Been fighting with your boyfriend, have you? Well, serves you right.' And with that he was gone.

The room was hot and clammy, but the spells of fever were gradually losing their grip. The bed squeaked like a concertina whenever I turned over, and after the net had come down three times, I let it lie where it was, sprawled over me, heavy and cumbersome, but at least quiescent. Strange noises filled the African night, tom-toms rumbled in the distance, jackals howled and screech-owls hooted, while the frogs added their deafening din to the general concert of the night. For three days and three nights, they kept me stewing in isolation, shrouded in my mosquito net like a moth caught in a spider's web. On the fourth day I was allowed to move to the balcony, where a dysentery case and a couple of nervous breakdowns were recovering under the open sky. For the first time I saw that we were on top of a hill which rolled gently down to the sea, just visible over the top of olive groves and cork oak trees.

For the next week I lay there, basking in the sun during the day, and under the shooting stars at night, in a blissful state of suspended animation. People drove out from Algiers, and brought me whatever books they could scrape up, and bits of gossip from our unit. Max Wilde became an inmate, and when he had sufficiently recovered from whatever ailed him, he came over from the men's ward to pay me little visits, which I returned with equal courtesy when I was allowed up, and we played lively games of poker with his ward-mates. Among them was a young pilot officer who had been shot down at Anzio, and though his hands were horribly burned, he was longing to get back to his squadron before the war came to an end. A couple of years later I met him again at the Lido airfield in Venice, and he was furious because the war was over, and he was put onto footling little jobs like flying my CO and myself down to Padua, in an Auster observation plane.

Although the hospital rations were no worse than in the Mess, I had lost weight and looked hideously scraggy. Captain Borden, catching sight of me on my return to the Mess, kindly suggested I should have a few days' convalescent leave before going back to work, and Maria booked me a room at our station in Bou-Saada in the desert. The PWB courier, a three-ton lorry, drove out twice a week with supplies, mail and personnel, and as there was one leaving the next day, I was told to get onto that.

One of our girls, who had contracted an American baby and suffered the horrors of abortion, was also on board. As her morale was very low and mine was soaring, I tried to share some of my overflowing excitement with her, but this only added to her asperity and irritation, so I joined in a game of poker with a couple of GIs on top of the mail and supply bags.

It took all day to drive the 250 kilometres to Bou-Saada, and as the sun climbed higher in the sky, the heat increased to an almost unbearable degree. The game of poker fizzled out, and I swung my legs over the edge of the lorry, watching the landscape roll away behind us, and the clouds of dust boiling up from under our wheels. The lush market-garden area south of Algiers, where the farmers were beginning to restore some order into their war-ruined fields and bombed-out vineyards, was gradually giving way to arid, stony palm groves sheltering Bedouin encampments, and as we drew nearer to the desert, all vegetation finally petered out, until only a few scorched and desiccated date palms stuck out of the stony ground, etched against the sky like dehydrated kipper backbones. And then, glory of glories, a caravan of camels undulating along the track, standing out in black against the setting sun, and making its way to the market of Bou-Saada. Tired, dusty and thirsty though I was after eight hours of bumping along in the three-tonner, I felt fulfilled and utterly content. This week in the desert was going to be one of utter bliss, and I wished with all my heart that I could make poor Tessa feel the same way. She was looking pale and hopeless, and by now I knew that there was nothing I could do to cheer her up. Grief and despair had really got their claws into her.

The holiday camp was as spartan as the hospital I had just left. The bedroom I was to share with a girl whose real name I never knew, but who liked to be called Cherry Blossom, contained two army cots and an orange box to be shared between us as a bedside table. It was a great treat to have a bed to yourself, after all these months, so that the bare gloomy bulb surrounded by a sombre cloud of flies and the cracked linoleum on the floor mattered very little by comparison. We feasted that night on cold bully and lettuce, the first green live thing I had tasted since I arrived in Algiers, the usual dog biscuits, and clusters of dry dates, which is the way they come fresh from the trees.

Cherry Blossom, who had been there a few days already and was obviously the self-appointed cheer-leader of the establishment, had ordered all the officers present to take off their pips, in order to do away with any stiffness or awkwardness among them. Nobody knew who was what, so that the youngest subaltern could chat up an elderly officer (who might be anything from a brigadier downwards) without undue deference. All of which made for a much more chummy atmosphere.

Dog-tired and shaky after the long drive, I crawled upstairs straight after dinner. As I lay on the wire bed which I had dragged out on the balcony I could hear, above the chorus of the frogs, the growling jackals fighting over choice morsels of refuse which littered the streets. Downstairs the assembled company, freed from the tyranny of their pips, were carousing in the bar, lustily singing *Lily Marlene* under the direction of Cherry Blossom.

Suddenly the door burst open and the light was switched on. I sat up in bed on my balcony. The young bombardier who was in charge of the reception desk was standing in the middle of the floor.

'What on earth is the matter?' I asked in alarm.

'You've got an officer in the room, miss, and it's against the rules.'

'Whatever are you talking about?' I squeaked, feeling outraged. 'Where do you think I could hide anyone in this room, and anyway what business have you of accusing me of breaking the rules? Who is in charge here?'

'The Mess Officer is out, miss, and I distinctly saw an officer coming upstairs when you left the dining-room.'

'Good God, Bombardier, is that all you've got to go by?'

'In this place it usually means one thing, miss.'

'Well search the room, and don't forget to look under the mattress,' I said, climbing out of bed. 'And then get the hell out of here, or I will report you to the Mess Officer in the morning.' I wouldn't have thought it possible, but believe it or not, the thick-headed youth, carrying out what he saw as his duty, actually peered inside and underneath the bed, at which I couldn't help laughing.

'Sorry I disturbed you, miss,' he finally said, and plodded out of the room, with his tail between his legs.

For the next couple of days I couldn't resist teasing him on my way up to bed.

'Am I to expect another visit from you tonight, Bombardier?' at which he blushed tomato-red and dived behind the reception desk.

In the daytime we strolled along the little streets, which were just dust lanes between the sand-coloured huts, and poked about among the carpet stores, the silver shops and the leather workers, who hammered and tooled their wares, squatting in the street outside their shops. One evening Cherry Blossom organised a cabaret of belly dancers for us, and young girls of about fourteen put on a fantastically exotic show. Another day she laid on a coach tour to Biskra (goodness knows how she got hold of the lorry to take us there) and a dozen of us set off for a long scorching day in the desert. I was glad to see that Tessa, who had palled up with a blond and decent, rather than good-looking, young subaltern, had perked up considerably and was looking much more cheerful. We passed several camps of Nomads, who seemed to do nothing but squat outside their tents waiting for passing trade. A couple of years before, when the Allies had landed in Africa, my husband told me later that, as they bowled along the coast road with the Eighth Army, women lined the way, selling cups of mother's milk.

We swopped cigarettes with our Nomads for ordinary goat cheese, and some of the famous Deglet en Nour dates, which are said to be the only ones without a worm in their hearts.

On the last day of my stay, the locusts came up from the south. The first warning we had of their approach was a black cloud slowly fanning out into the sky from the distant horizon. It was fascinating to watch their advance. The noise they produced was like an approaching bomber squadron. Within an hour of their first appearance they were with us, churning all round with this extraordinary roaring sound, settling on anything handy, creeping through your hair, and dropping to the ground where they were crunched underfoot until all the streets were running with a pulpy, squashy, squelchy mush of crushed locust. All day they milled around, until at sunset they dropped out of the sky and tucked themselves up for the night several feet deep over the town.

Locusts travel only by day and feed at night, when you can hear the champing of their jaws for miles around. In the morning the little vegetable plots were cropped down to the roots, a pathetic, dilapidated sight, and the locusts, having sucked the oasis dry in a few hours, took to the air again at dawn. We all set off together, and they escorted us back to the coast. By the time we arrived at nightfall, they had already roosted in Algiers, and a hundred or so of these prickly customers crawled into bed with me when I finally got there. They were swarming again the next day when we woke up. The sun was obliterated, and we had to have breakfast by electric light. Getting to work was a ticklish problem, as they lay a foot deep over the town steps. After several attempts at negotiating this hazard, we beat a hasty retreat back to the Mess, and Major Twist organised a fleet of cars and lorries to convey us to our various offices. It was a squelchy, crunchy journey, with the windscreen wipers working overtime on the squashed insects trickling down the windows. Everywhere at street corners, Arabs had set up little charcoal stoves like chestnut roasters, and they were tossing locusts into frying pans, and selling them in little cornets of paper to the passing crowd. I didn't actually taste any, but Dr Livingstone, who obviously had, has written that, dipped in honey, they are far more delicious than shrimps and mayonnaise.

In Basic News the Editor was tearing his hair. Everything on the big central table was on the move. You couldn't put a sheet of paper down without it being immediately carried away by a battalion of locusts who bore it along on their little shoulders to some totally unexpected spot. Typewriters were gummed up with the creatures who had spent the night in the works, so that the minute you began to hit the keys, thick juicy jets of minced-up locust squirted off in all directions. This went on for three days. On the fourth they were gone, all except for the littered streets, and the obscured window panes against which so many had crashed and disintegrated.

Above: *Basic News* in Algiers. A solid hour was spent tidying up the usual mess for the benefit of the photographer.

Below: The oasis of Bou-Saada before the locust invasion.

Above: Nomads in the desert waiting for passing trade.

Below: Christmas Day in Rome, 1944. Joy, Jan and myself
with our escorts.

Above: Rome, 1944. Dinner at the Nirvanetta Club with an officer on leave from the Gothic Line.

Below: The hill town of Cassino, bastion of the German Gustav line, begins to crumble under fire of the Allied Fifth Army. Above it on the hill is the ancient Benedictine monastery, believed to have been used by the Germans as an artillery position and observation post.

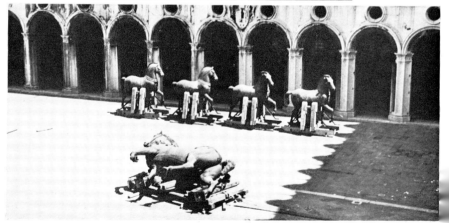

Above: Setting up the type for the *Salerno Times* during the landings. Captain Beauclerk calmly smokes his pipe under heavy enemy shelling.

Centre: Firing leaflets in two-inch mortar smoke-bombs over the line at Alife di Piedimonte.

Below: The horses of Venice, coming out of hiding, return to their immemorial perches.

Above left: The RAF fly-past to celebrate the uncovering of San Marco's face which had been boarded up during the war.

Above right: The law court in Venice. At the Allied table in the background Major Coates-Preedy is on the right and I am on the left.

Below left: Trieste in August, 1945. Sitting on the rocks in the sun.

Below right: With officers of the 56th Division under canvas on the Morgan Line.

Above: The officers on the bridge never took their eyes off the surface of the sea.

Below: Shooting up the released mines which have popped up to the surface.

Above left: The mine-sweeping fleet in action in the Adriatic.

Above right: A mine floating loose before being blown up by the ship's guns.

Below: An Italian mine, released from its mooring, is hauled up to the Captain's ship for inspection.

Above: Mine-spotting on the bridge with the Captain.

Below: Vienna, 1945. Max Wilde is chatting up one of his Soviet friends.

5

In Algiers, where we crouched over our typewriters, anxiously waiting for the first trickle of news, the sun rose unconcernedly in a delicate mother-of-pearl sky, as Overlord thundered into action on the North-west coast of France.

The greatest armada in the history of the world was on its way across the English Channel, almost a thousand years after William the Conqueror, going the opposite way, had landed his troops on the beaches of Southern England. Over five thousand ships of every size, shape and description, including ancient cargoes, channel steamers, passenger boats, tankers and hospital ships, were used to convey the troops across the sea. The Americans advanced in twenty-one stately convoys, while the British and Canadian Task Force numbered thirty-eight, all of which had set off in complete secrecy from their assembly point south of the Isle of Wight at dead of night, while overhead roared twelve thousand aircraft with their gigantic load of airborne troops.

The majestic fleet advanced in orderly, prearranged lanes, with everyone in his prescribed place, while hundreds of motor-launches buzzed up and down the aisles like agitated sheepdogs. But the weather was breaking up and the Channel waters, as if they sensed the vast menace which brooded upon the surface, heaved and stirred uneasily. Soon, huge waves crashed over the sides of the shallow landing craft in which the men, packed like sardines, and hardly able to stretch their legs, were soaked to the skin. Cold, stiff with cramp and apprehensive, knowing full well that many of them would never see another sunrise, a great number were sea-sick all through the night as well. But in spite of the misery of this crossing, and their exhausted and washed-out arrival on the beaches, they fought like demons to establish a foothold, through the barbed wire, the underwater obstacles, the sea-defences and the mines, and continual vicious firing from the coast.

Between Vierville and Colville, the stretch which the Americans called Omaha Beach, the German sea-defences were heavily covered by a multitude of guns tucked away and concealed among the dunes. Fearful of all these fireworks, the Americans had decided to unload their troops into beach landing craft twelve miles away from the shore. As the sea was now running high, a great number of these small boats, designed only for the shallows, and washed over by enormous waves, sank hopelessly to the bottom, while many of the soldiers, dragged down by their heavy equipment, were drowned, or swept far away from their objective. Covering fire from the US warships was either aimed too high, over the heads of the beach defences, with shells blowing the sand of the dunes harmlessly into the sky, while others, exploding on the beach, wreaked terrible havoc among their own men.

The appalling confusion of the landings, and the pitiful number of casualties led the Germans to believe they had won the day, and at noon they optimistically but prematurely announced victory. They were, however, counting without the incredible determination and heroic courage of American troops once they have got the bit between their teeth. As so often happened, the men on the spot made up by their tenacity for the bungling of their leaders. Veterans from Sicily and Salerno, whose shining spirit was armour-plated against ordinary human fear, wading stolidly through minefields, pushed inland, and by nightfall there were over thirty-four thousand men firmly established on shore.

Compared with this particular beachhead, which had hung in the balance for many hours, the other landings were smooth and harmonious exercises. The British and Canadian Divisions, admirably covered by faultless firing from the Royal Navy, and following in the tracks of fleets of Sherman tanks cunningly adapted and bristling with a multiplicity of protective extensions, such as flailing arms to set off mines, raced inland and had reached the outskirts of Bayeux by the evening.

But before any of these landings were to take place, a great deal of essential softening up had occurred inland at dead of night, carried out by the airborne divisions. In the Cherbourg area, American volunteer parachutists came down soon after midnight to mark dropping zones for the twelve thousand paratroops who were to follow one hour later. The 'Pathfinders', as they were called, unfortunately encountering heavy firing, had been scattered far and wide. But in spite of this they had managed to capture their objective of Sainte Mère Église and Pouppeville. These heroic young men, and sixty volunteers of the 6th British Airborne Division dropped near Caen, were said by Cornelius Ryan in his book *The Longest Day* to have had 'one of the toughest of D-Day jobs'.

Landing in total darkness in unknown territory, the Red Devil volunteers, as the 6th Airborne was known, had exactly half an hour to find their bearings, locate the appointed zones, and mark them up with flares and radar equipment to guide the main British airborne troops to their landing stage. This territory, which lay in a twenty-mile radius, formed a triangle between Varaville, Ranville and Touffreville.

The first lot, who were exceptionally lucky, floated down almost on top of their target. The Ranville contingent were welcomed with heavy ack-ack fire which scattered them far and wide, while the Touffreville party, jumping into an unexpected wind, lost six of their men who were helplessly swept away towards the flooded Dives River valley, where they were pitifully drowned in three feet of water, tangled in their chutes and dragged down by the weight of their equipment.

In the first Pathfinder plane of the Touffreville detachment, my brother John, huddled with eleven other volunteers, impatiently awaited his turn, while the first man, stuck in the drophole with his folding bicycle, struggled to get free. When he eventually managed to get through, and the others were able to follow, the plane was already several miles away from their objective, towards which they had to double back on their mini-bikes in complete darkness.

My cousin Louis, who had saved a place in his own Pathfinder for John, as they had long ago decided to fly over together, had to go without him in the end, as John was detailed at the last minute before leaving England 'to do another job'. And that is all I am allowed to say about it. Which was perhaps just as well after all, since poor Louis, one of the hundred and fifty volunteers who stormed the German battery at Merville, was taken prisoner within a few hours.

In Basic News, the Editor, who was rifling through a pile of press photographs, tossed one across the table. 'Say, baby, is that guy anything to do with you? Same name.'

'Yes,' I answered, bursting with pride. 'It's my brother.' There, before my eyes, stood John, with one arm in a sling, in the ploughed-up street of a village in ruins, surrounded by a section of parachutists, while the caption said, 'Sergeant Fesq of Field Security, 6th Airborne Division, was mentioned in despatches for outstanding gallantry in action.'

Although we had been up all night, and I had only managed to snatch a couple of hours' sleep on the floor of Home's kitchen, the noise and bustle, and continual stream of bulletins and flashes incessantly pouring in over our instruments, kept us hopping with excitement, noticing neither the heat nor lack of sleep. For several hours, in fact until noon, it was impossible to form any clear idea of the layout and advance on the various beachheads, and all we could do was simply to churn out the incoherent information as it reached us over the air.

By the evening, a pattern began to emerge. US General Pratt had been killed in the unfortunate glider landings of the 101st Unit, most of which were wrecked, while the 82nd, largely brought in by inexperienced pilots, crashed into hedgerows, buildings, rivers and marshes, with eighteen pilots killed on landing. Their scattered equipment was too damaged to be of use to anybody.

Of the sixty-nine English gliders in the Caen area, forty-nine touched down on the correct strip. Although many of them broke up on landing, there were few casualties. The bridges over the Orne River, which were their objective, were stormed and captured within fifteen minutes, while the sleepy German guards were still struggling into their boots. By evening, all the positions were firmly held.

It was a great triumph, and evident to a jubilant world, that the end was now in sight. Monty, who always required a vast arena in which to deploy his talents, was in his element once more, cleverly exploiting the national charactcristics of the troops under his command, and therefore getting the best out of them. Pinning a large German force down in Caen with fourteen British Divisions, he provided a breakthrough for the US troops, who galloped on to overrun Brittany. After the German counterattack on Avranches on 7 August, the Fifth Panzer and the Seventh Armies found themselves trapped, with fifty thousand taken prisoner and ten thousand killed. But Hitler, still holding out, was convinced that the Allies would scrap among themselves and give up the fight, when already well within sight of victory! Still following the advice of his unlucky stars, and conducting great battles at their bidding, he simply could not see the facts as they were. Blinded by Astrology, he blundered daily deeper into disaster.

Meanwhile in Basic News the pace was slowing down on the night shift, as we grew used to the spectacular advances of the Allied armies. So much now did we take constant success for granted, that a reverse was unthinkable. The Editor, leaving me once more in charge of the night shift, resumed his interrupted social life. I was able to go home after the midnight communiqué again, and was back on the Madrague run most mornings.

In the little officers' Mess on the beach, the Old Men's talk lost some of its fascination when two new friends, David and Elliot, joined us. Active and restless, they could hardly wait to finish their last mouthful to be up and away, walking briskly along the shore, with me trotting after them like a dog at their heels. Their own particular brand of nonsense, in the tradition of the Marx Brothers, I found completely irresistible. They rattled on in a rapid give and take of perpetual non-sequiturs. It was like a very lively game of ping-pong with the ball forever in the air and never touching the table. Anything was grist to their mill. A couple of decrepit old Arabs, crouching on the beach like sacks of coal, in their sand-coloured burnouses, with a scraggy hen on the end of a long thin string, pecking about among the seaweed, would set them off on an imaginary conversation of pure lunacy between the men and their hen. Or a wild-eyed seagull, clutching a tuft of yellow straw sticking out of either side of its beak like the bedraggled whiskers of an angry Brigadier, caught their fancy, and away they went, while I plodded after them barefoot, straining not to miss a word, and laughing until my ribs ached. But it wasn't only on the beach that they indulged in their favourite pastime. When the devil got into them, they would put on a show in the bar of the Aletti Hotel in Algiers, next to a tableful of high-ranking officers from AFHQ, who bristled and glared in outraged disapproval, at which I became so hysterical that I had to stagger off to the *Dames* to recover, with tears rolling down my face. In restaurants, they would switch from English to French for the benefit of the unhappy waiters, who were driven out of their wits by all the crazy nonsense.

After Maria had left for Naples with Major Twist and his circus, to conduct the affairs of PWB in Italy, I had the bed to myself for a whole night. Getting a taste for this untoward luxury, I was quite put out the next afternoon when I came up to change after a long day at the Madrague, to find a pile of elegant white calfskin cases stacked on the bed. But by the next morning I was delighted with this new arrival. Jan, who was about my age, was the daughter of a physician from Boston. Her clothes, even everyday blouses and skirts, were all expensive models, which made my own curious assortment of garments appear odder still, even to myself. Jan looked like a Giotto angel, with pale butter-coloured hair fluffed out around a perfect oval face, dark-brown eyes and jet-black eyebrows and lashes. The Cats' Club of the Unit, with their sharp and bitter tongues, proclaimed it all to be artificial, which I indignantly refuted. Jan was a sweet-natured, serious-minded girl, entirely devoid of guile, and there was absolutely nothing artificial about her. The morning after her arrival, I bounced into the office. 'Thank you, dear Loot, for my nice new room-mate,' I said gratefully.

'I thought the two of you would make a good pair,' he answered. Dear man, I could have hugged him, when I thought of all the Miriams at large in the Mess. In PWB you were *awfully* dependent on the other person in your bed.

Hardly able to wait and show her off to Elliott and David, I bore her off to lunch with them that very day. David fell in love with her on the spot, a contingency which simply hadn't occurred to me and would, I thought with dismay, wreck our cosy set-up for ever more. But far from this happening, it just became a new subject for David's fertile inventive brain, and he straightaway slid into the role of the comic lover, taking himself off and commenting on his own feelings as if he were sending up a total and rather absurd stranger. Elliott took up the cue, and the hilarious dialogue which bounced back and forth between them kept Jan and me in constant fits. She enjoyed the show as much as I did.

Those last three weeks in Algiers were magical. As a *real* Captain (Jan and I being 'assimilated' ones) David could always produce a car and chauffeur, and we drove off with a bag of dog biscuits from the Mess, and doughnuts and cans of beer contributed by Elliott from the PX. Armed with these iron rations, we sometimes went inland into the foothills of the Atlas mountains as far as we dared, where the tombs of prophets and holy men brooded under ancient cedars and eucalyptus trees, and unfriendly tribes glared, daring us to go further.

On the whole, the coast was our favourite run, and we poked about among Roman remains, ruined villages and tiny fishing ports tucked away among the rocks. Tipasa, seventy miles west of Algiers, had been a larger and more important harbour than Carthage at the height of Phoenician prosperity. Its particular position on the map made it an ideal spot for overland and maritime trade, which all greedy invaders hanker after, and so it was conquered by the Romans, overrun by the Vandals, captured by the Byzantines, and liberated by the Muslims. All had left their mark in the shape of tomb, necropolis, basilica, amphitheatre and forum, the whole overgrown with asphodel, wild thyme, lentisk, carob trees and here and there the odd gnarled olive, dignified palm and turpentine pine.

There had been no rain for five months, and under the constant raging inferno of the sun, the ground crackled underfoot like dry toast. Snakes basked on the rough broken seats of the auditorium, and tough little orchids with an overpowering scent pushed their way through the cracks in the scorching stone, while enormous green lizards glared at us, with their throats gulping and throbbing with speechless anger at our intrusion. The crumbs we threw them were pounced upon by enormous glistening black ants with claws like forceps and huge muscular thighs, and giant furry hornets dived at your face, crashed on their bellies and backpedalled in confusion. The asphodels, now past their prime and fermenting on the stalk, gave out a pungent intoxicating odour competing sharply with the acrid smell oozing out of the pine trees. And above everything else droned the syncopated drumming of the cicada chorus, like the muffled thud of a huge and all-embracing heartbeat pounding up out of the earth.

The brain inside my skull, scrambled to a pulp by the heat of the sun and the effect of the beer, was spinning out a succession of pictures like a reel of technicolour film. Sizzling luxuriously on the hot stone, I could see the bustle of motley crowds milling about in the harbour, curiously clothed swarthy little men with curly black beards, waving their arms and shouting above the general uproar, sailors jumping on and off their boats, dressed in little skirts and skull caps, flinging ropes at one another, while girls in long striped tunics minced about with baskets on their heads. Equally vivid were the crowds in the Forum, and the groups of dignified self-conscious-looking men in togas and Roman haircuts. The boom of Gregorian chanting came from the Basilica, mingling with the agonised screams of men whose hands and tongues were cut out by the hordes of Huneric, who thundered about on his ferocious little Tartar mount, urging his men to yet more fearful atrocities. In the harbour the water bubbled and boiled with the blood of the little martyr who had been thrown into it, refusing to simmer down until her body had been fished out and given a decent burial.

Overwhelmed by my visions and the heat, I crept down to the rocks and slipped into the tepid glass-clear water. The delicious feeling of plenitude which usually comes with a very high tide pervaded the little harbour. No dig had ever taken place at Tipasa. Untold archaeological treasures lay under a few inches of sand. Broken urns, huge chains encrusted with barnacles, ancient strangely shaped anchors lay under a thin film of silt and weed. I swam around close to the bottom, followed by bright blue fish darting around in shoals. The sun, shining on their backs, caused wavy little shadows to skim along ahead on the sandy bottom. Jan and the boys soon followed me into the water, and we chased and splashed one another until quite exhausted, and it was time to think of getting back.

On the journey home Jan, who was unusually relaxed, let herself go to the extent of singing American ditties to us. We were spellbound by her clear high voice. It was like the singing of a choir boy, and belonged under the echoing roof of a cathedral. Poor David, staring out of the window, had great fat tears rolling down his face. I longed to hug and comfort him, but I knew quite well that there was nothing I could do. Before anyone else could notice he had managed to recover, and resume his customary tomfool nonsense with Elliott.

In the hurly-burly of the Mess a shy, serious-looking young American Captain went about his business with a calm composure very different from the usual drunken, noisy, harum-scarum wildness of the rest of my colleagues. Sometimes, as I gobbled my dinner before rushing back to Basic News for the night shift, he came and sat next to me, crumbling dog biscuits in silence all over the table-cloth, and then just as I was hurtling down the stairs, he would start playing the piano in a most tantalising way. Strains of Schubert, or some tinkling Mozart sonata would come wafting after me, and I couldn't help feeling that if ever we had the chance, we could become good friends. In the end, it was his Colonel who broke the ice between us. 'C'mon, you two,' he said one evening that I was off duty, and we were eating at the same table in the Mess, 'I'm going to the Officers' Club, and I'm taking the two of you along.' And we all piled into his station-wagon.

The August night being hot and sticky, we sat in the courtyard, drinking iced limejuice (they had rum in theirs) and watched in silence the unhappy cabaret going through their antics on a tiny one-wheeled bicycle. My companions being very thirsty, the drinks came and went at an increas-ing rate. The Colonel was soon past all speech (being normally so saturated, that it took little to top him up) and my Captain was beginning to open up a bit at last. He was talking about his wonderful German mother. I lis-tened with one ear, while lending the other to the witti-cisms of the artistes on the dance floor. Suddenly I realised that he was edging up and panting down my ear. Oh dear, I thought, he is sloshed before we've had a chance of get-ting to know each other.

'You're a nice girl,' he hiccupped down my neck. 'I always thought so, and now I know.' (Whatever made him think so, I wondered, shuddering at the thought, who the hell wanted to be a dreary thing like that?) 'My mother would like you, you know,' he added fatuously. I nearly groaned aloud, as my heart silently slid into the Slough of Despond. He won't do, he just won't do, I thought sadly to myself.

'Tell me about your job,' I suggested, losing all interest.

'Well, what do you know?' he exclaimed in surprise. 'She wants to know about my job!'

'Well, why don't you tell me about it?'

'If I told you I could get shot, that's why.'

'For heaven's sake,' I said in alarm. 'Don't tell me, then.' But warmed up as he was by the pernicious rum, there was no holding him back now that he was wound up.

'Just to show how much I trust you, I will tell you, whether you like it or not.' And creeping up nearer still, he breathed damply into my ear, 'I'm working on Operation Dragoon.'

'Whatever's that?' I asked, intrigued.

'It's what used to be called Anvil, until the Germans got wise to it. It's the invasion of the South of France,' he hissed impressively.

My heart gave a great lurch. I clutched his arm, 'Oh you don't mean it!' I exclaimed, choking with excitement. 'When?'

'Fifteenth of August is D-Day, and now I'll get shot for telling you,' he repeated, with a slight attack of Conscience.

'No you won't, because I'll never tell. But I'm so, so glad to hear about it.'

'I thought you would be. I shouldn't have told you, but I know you won't rat on me.' After the first few moments of excitement, I realised the folly of his confidence. If ever I were nabbed, I knew I would spill the beans at the first turn of the screw, and from that moment on until D-Day, I lived in perpetual dread of being kidnapped, a possibility which had never occurred to me before.

On the night of the fourteenth, none of us went to bed at all, and the state of excitement in Basic News was even greater than for the Normandy landings. Many of our friends were in the show, and as it was taking place on the opposite shore, we felt closely involved, and for me of course it was the liberation of my childhood home. Impatiently waiting for the first trickle of news, their nerves on edge, the journalists swore and cursed each other with rich colourful oaths. I kept well out of the way. At eleven o'clock the Editor sent a couple of GIs to the PX for sustenance. They returned with two buckets of coffee and several bags of doughnuts, and masses of paper cups.

Only the dullest news was coming over the machines, General Alexander pushing up north of Rome, the Germans retreating from Argentan on the Western Front, all good expected daily stuff we had now got used to, our armies moving forward on every front. But still nothing from Dragoon! I grew drowsier as the night progressed. It was terribly hot, with little individual heat waves coming out of each machine, and great torrid breaths puffing in through the windows from the furnace of the street below. The entire insect population of the town came cruising into this inviting atmosphere, making straight for the lamp over the table, into which they inevitably crashed. At about two in the morning, as I could keep awake no longer, I decided to make myself a nest in the midst of a huge pile of wood shavings, and in a few minutes, in spite of the noise, the smells, the swearing and the heat, I was fast asleep. It seemed only a minute later that a great clamour brought me back to life.

'They've landed ... they've made it!' Everybody was shouting. I leapt to the teleprinters, trailing wood shavings across the floor. The beaches between Cap Nègre and Agay were covered with disembarking troops. General Patch's three Divisions were wading ashore at Cavalaire, Pampelone, Sainte Maxime, Fréjus and Le Drammont. During the night parachutists had landed behind the range of the Maure mountains, and French Partisans had paralysed enemy batteries on the heights, creeping up on them from behind with blackened faces, bits of thyme in their tin hats and a knife between their teeth in true commando style. As there was practically no resistance, there was disappointingly little news. Five hundred thousand men, two hundred and thirty warships and fifteen thousand aircraft, finding themselves slightly disconcerted by the remarkable facility of the operation, went through it all like butter. And that was in spite of a subtle and ingenious plan, devised by the Admiralty in London, falling flat on its face at the last minute. A French-speaking officer of the RNVR, specially selected for his flawless accent and engaging manner, had been sent out to Algiers specifically to prepare the ground for the landings. He was to wade ashore, waving his gun in the air shouting 'Ne tirez pas, nous sommes Americains.' The idea being that the Americans, having had nothing to do with the sinking of the French fleet at Toulon, would be welcome, whereas the British might get a hot reception for their villainy.

On arriving in Algiers, the gallant sailor naturally went to seek out his friends and bring the good news. Overjoyed, the friends called in the neighbours who brought along *their* chums, so that an enormous and convivial party was soon in progress, celebrating the morrow's invasion of the South of France, and to hell with security. The sailor was busy preparing the ground on the spot, but that is, alas, as far as he got. The next morning, about five hours after the troops had splashed their way ashore across the shallows on the other side of the sea, he found himself, to his great surprise, waking up in a strange bed with a buxom lady he had never seen in his life before.

Meanwhile we were standing at double strength in Basic News, expecting a non-stop stream of flashes and bulletins of engagements, counter-attacks, advance and retreat, as had poured out of the Western Front on the day of the Normandy landings. After the great build-up, it was all falling a little flat. But we were none the less making the most of it, extracting every possible ounce of drama from the situation.

The newsmen, bleary-eyed with whisky and lack of sleep, and bristling with unshaven jaws, banged about, shouting and swearing and doing their best to work up an atmosphere. After all, this was a great significant moment, we were writing living history! The Editor, still rooted to the middle of the floor, where he may have stood all night while I slumbered in my wood shavings, was buried up to the hocks in reams of yellow teleprinter despatches. We were all banging away merrily at our type-writers, but it was mostly the same story coming over the air from AP, UP, Reuters, OWI, MOI and so on. I was doing the straight stuff for the radio, and the boys were putting in the sobs for their audience in the States. And suddenly a couple of freshly laundered GIs came in bearing between them a pail of coffee, followed by Dandelion and Sweet Pea laden with sandwiches and doughnuts. It was a welcome sight. Falling upon this manna, I helped the girls to distribute breakfast, then settled down to it myself. Everything looked up after that, and the lack of gory battles, and the disappointingly easy win fell into perspec-tive, and I realised the wonder and the mercy of the whole bloodless operation. It had taken five days and five nights to assemble the enormous Task Force of Operation Dragoon, and the Germans had had absolutely no inkling of what was going on. We could at least make the most of that.

For the next four days we were pretty solidly on duty, avidly soaking up every little scrap coming over from the South of France and rejoicing noisily with the help of rivers of gin and Scotch, at the complete rout of the enemy, who scrabbled inland as fast as he could go, while those who couldn't make it were mopped up in the liberation of Marseilles, where General de Lattre de Tassigny popped a cool thirty-five thousand Germans into the bag. General

Eisenhower, to justify this little caper, jubilantly declared it to be 'the most decisive contribution to the complete defeat of the Germans'.

Considering everything, this thrust into the soft underbelly of Europe, which had originally been meant to coincide with the Normandy landings and draw enemy troops away from there, and which had been the cause of so much bitter wrangling among the generals, accomplished very little in the end, except to prolong the war in Italy for almost another year. General Alexander, whose forces were struggling inch by inch up the length of Italy against a desperate enemy, superior in arms and numbers, if not in fighting spirit, protested vehemently against losing so many of his badly needed troops, to swell the ranks of Dragoon. But Churchill was overruled by Eisenhower, who was bulldozed by President Roosevelt. In the end, it was a question of politics. When it eventually came to the crunch, and an overwhelmingly crushing argument had to be found to persuade Churchill, Roosevelt came out with what seemed to me an astounding revelation. It appeared that he would not survive the coming elections if it became known in the States that even the slightest reverse on the Western Front were due to troops being kept in Italy to help Alexander win through to the Po Valley!

6

WHEN ALL THE excitement was over, there was very little left for us to do. The war in Africa being concluded, AFHQ moved to the Palace of Caserta near Naples, and PWB Algiers drifted over the sea in small sections, to roost in Naples, which was to be the next HQ. Our Editor decided to give us a closing-down party in Basic News. It was, as usual, a terribly hot night, and all the insect life of Algiers was making itself at home, zooming and buzzing around the room. We felt sad, dispossessed, unwanted, superfluous, and on an occasion like this, no one was going to remain sober long. In fact it was a point of honour to arrive already well lit-up. Scotch had been generously donated by the British denizens of the Mess, and it was flowing steadily down all those thirsty American gullets. Dandelion, Sweet Pea and I were kept busy filling glasses. The noise was growing, as well as the excitement, and the general pathos of the situation. Wherever you looked, tears stood in little pink screwed-up eyes, and from time to time a choking voice croaked, 'Gee, Spike (or Hank, or Kurt or Chant, or whatever), I reckon we had some pretty good times here, didn't we?'

'C'mon, you guys,' said someone on a sudden inspiration, 'let's give 'em a tickertape reception down there,' and he hurled an armful of typing paper over the balcony. Nobody needed much encouragement after that. Every available scrap was flung out, and when no paper was left, empty whisky bottles followed suit. Rather apprehensively, I peered over the edge to count the casualties, but dimly lit though it was, the street appeared to be empty. Nobody in their senses would hang around below while Basic News was having a party. Everything detachable went overboard. When the telephone extensions were wrenched out of the walls and tipped over the side, I felt the time had come for me to take my leave.

None of the newsmen appeared at breakfast the next day. The Editor was nowhere to be found. Basic News was a scene of total devastation. Not a soul was around. I trotted over to see Captain Borden, who was packing the office files into crates with the aid of a corporal and a couple of privates.

'Take a few days off,' he suggested. 'Then get yourself to Naples; report to Major Twist when you arrive there.'

'But how shall I get there? I need travel orders.'

'So you do. Come round tomorrow morning, and I'll have them ready for you. And now get out of my hair, there's a good girl.'

When I got back rather disconsolately from his office, the Madrague Mail was standing outside the Mess. The German Jewish contingent being already on board, the Hungarian sergeant fixed a mournful eye upon me. 'You might as well come to the beach with us. There's nothing else to do.' So for the next few days, we went to the Madrague, more to keep out of the way than anything else. But it wasn't the same any longer. We were restless, unsettled, and I could understand the way swallows must feel when the time for emigrating is upon them. One morning I decided that this had come, packed my kitbag, picked up my bear, paid my Mess bill, and hitch hiked to Maison Blanche Airport.

The heat of the sun coming off the tarmac of the airstrip almost took your breath away. It was like trying to walk around in a hot frying pan. With the bear under my arm and dragging my kitbag, I panted over to an empty hangar. An RAF corporal was inside, reading a comic in the sultry gloom.

'Anything going to Naples today?' I asked hopefully.

'Not that I know of, love. You want to go there?'

'I have to go. Do you know when anyone's going?'

'Not a clue, sweetheart. Better ask the Station Commander.'

The SC's stooge, when I finally tracked him down, said yes, he thought there was a Dakota going over the next morning.

'Do you think they would give me a lift?'

'Nothing to do with me, miss. Better ask the pilot.' The third Dakota on whose door I knocked turned out to be the one. 'Why not? Hop in,' said the pilot hospitably, in answer to my request. 'I was going to take the old crate over tomorrow to pick up a load of wounded, but I'll fly you over now if you're in a hurry. Besides, it will be cooler up there.' The heat of the cabin nearly knocked me out. 'Come along up front, there's nobody else on board. Got a movement order, I take it?'

'Yes, do you want to see it?'

'No thanks, squeeze in here.' And I squatted between him and the co-pilot, with the bear on my knee.

We had understandably sweltered on African soil, but it was still almost as hot up in the clear, cool-looking heights of the sky. The temperature was still in the eighties, and a KD shirt was all we could bear on our backs.

When I asked my husband recently why he had chosen such a sordid old dump as the Singer building for PWB

HQ when he had arrived in Naples with the Eighth Army, he answered, 'There weren't many buildings left standing after the bombing and the shelling, you know, and most of what was left was bagged by other units. It was the best we could do, although I know it wasn't up to much.'

A dirtier, gloomier place I had never seen in my life, and when Maria, who was working there, poor soul, told me that Basic News had settled in Rome, my spirits rose considerably. 'You will have to find your way there, but stay here for a few days, and I will show you round.' Meanwhile, she produced a car (all these comforts were, as usual, at her beck and call) to whisk me up to the PWB Mess on the Vomero in the hills above Naples, overlooking the Bay. The famous view lived up to its reputation, and it was reassuring to see the Royal Navy keeping watch out there in strength. The Villa, which was totally bare, had obviously received the attentions of practised and experienced looters. The bedroom I was assigned contained six iron bedsteads with no mattresses, sheets or blankets. For an Officers' Mess, it was probably one of the most spartan in the town. But accommodation was never one of PWB's strong points.

A quick sortie into the surrounding bedrooms produced a couple of army blankets, which I spread on the wire bedstead next to the window, and in spite of the squeaks and the creaks and the cruel wire mesh, and the squads of diving mosquitoes, I slept like a dormouse all the time I was at the Villa Amphora.

Downstairs in the dining-room we feasted on Compo rations instead of the usual American fare, which meant that bully beef was substituted for the usual spam, a nice change, and instead of butter, the kind of margarine which had to be chipped off the old block and came away in brittle shavings, bouncing and rattling on the plate. And tea, of course, took the place of coffee.

Conveniently close to the Villa was the Orangerie

nightclub, where we had dinner on the terrace, with fairy lights in the orange trees, and the whole bay with its warships spread out below. The sharp smell of the trees and of the freshly watered nasturtiums and geraniums, puffing out their heady scent into the night air, gave the place a special flavour all of its own. Maria's fiancé, Andrew, whose Second Echelon was lodged at Caserta Palace cheek by jowl with AFHQ, joined Maria and myself, and brought along for my benefit a jaunty Scottish Major who swung his kilt with great panache. A good dancer, he was full of chat, gossip and high spirits. I met him again later in Rome, where we spent many a sweltering summer afternoon snaking our way around the cool labyrinths of the Catacombs. And then suddenly, mysteriously, he was dead. The sort of fate frequently in store for officers in the less regular forms of employment.

The time came, a few days later, when I began to feel restless, and thought I really ought to get down to work again, although Maria laughed at this unnatural and misguided desire on my part. 'You haven't seen Amalfi or Sorrento. You may never get the chance again.' But I did climb Vesuvius with the Scottish Major. We toiled to the top and stared down into the crater, where columns of steam oozed out of the cracks in the rocks, hundreds of feet below. It seemed incredible that this quiet and empty crater could ever belch out tons of red-hot rock and mud into the sky.

Two or three times a week, the PWB courier left Naples at noon loaded with mail, supplies, plus two or three passengers and their gear, aiming to reach Rome by 6 pm, which was the GI driver's dinner hour at his mess. If he didn't make it by then, he had to go without a meal. Highway 7, which followed the coast, full of potholes and bomb craters, was used by the courier as a racetrack. We flew along from bump to rut, leaping over the crags and the craters, taking to the air, and more often than not, landing on two wheels. Sometimes it was in the ditch, down a ravine or slap into a pile of bombed-out army vehicles. But we were constantly lucky on this trip. The driver, his mouth full of gum, was chewing the cud and swinging his jaws from side to side like an angry camel, rotating the wheel of the weapons carrier hand over hand, as he sprang and leapt about in his seat.

The rumour was that there were more casualties on the courier run than on the Gothic Line, and the PWB Mess in Rome was, as a result, continually crawling with limping, hopping and walking wounded. Broken necks and bashed-in ribcages retired into the hairy arms of a military hospital outside the town, and sometimes didn't reappear for several weeks.

With jubilation in my heart, I bounced along the ploughed-up highway, rejoicing in the knowledge of the German rout. This time *they* were on the run, and *we* in pursuit, the reverse of that other scorching summer four years ago, when we were fleeing before their Panzer divisions on the west coast of France. Since those days I have had some very good German friends, but I am talking of times of war, when the lid is lifted off the top of Hell, and all its nameless horrors crawl out, spreading their pollution in all directions, and insanity stalks the earth, warping the minds of men. And I was no exception to this universal contamination. If we had been chasing the Japanese, my exultation would have been even greater.

The countryside was totally ripped apart by war, the villages along the road annihilated into great anonymous heaps of dust and rubble. South of Terracina, the Pontine Marshes had flooded everything in sight, and malarial mosquitoes, subdued for so many years, had bounced vigorously back to life, indulging once more in an orgy of sex and egg-laying.

What wasn't actually under water had been taken over for army camps or parking space for mile upon mile of trucks, armoured cars, Bren-carriers, tanks and great guns slumbering under their canvas hoods, and everywhere lay the wreckage of burnt-out aircraft, blown-up tanks and other engines of war, twisted and tortured out of all recognition.

At Capua we crossed the Volturno over a Bailey Bridge, that very same Vulturnus where, in 215 BC, Hannibal had made such fools of the Romans who had encircled him, by sending two thousand head of cattle with flaming faggots between their horns galloping up the hill, to make it appear as if his troops had stampeded in a panic. There were in fact many similarities between the two great generals, Hannibal who had invaded from the north and Alexander who came up from the south. Both had the same indomitable courage and unyielding tenacity, the same total disregard for danger, imperturbability in tight corners, and what can only be called inventive genius in military matters. When everything was going wrong and the battle seemed lost, up popped some brilliant idea into their lively brains, as when Hannibal, who was plainly losing the battle against the Pergamum fleet, ordered pots full of poisonous snakes to be tossed over into the enemy ships, thereby causing an immediate and total rout.

Terracina, built at the foot of the mountains and directly on the seashore, must have been very seductive in its leisurely, unworried pre-war days, as yet undiscovered by the tourist trade and living entirely for fishing, sitting in the sun, singing and love. Now the place was in ruins, but the inhabitants, lounging and gossiping about among the rubble, hadn't moved a single stone, and children were climbing up to bed over great heaps of masonry to the first floor, which lay crumpled in the middle of the street, or lodged on top of the house next door. No attempt had been made to clear up, let alone rebuild anything. The people simply crept about among the ruins, like scorpions.

The fighting in the South, fearful and stupefying in its

unremitting intensity, was mostly conducted in appalling weather, endless downpours of rain, and a perpetual swaying sea of mud, several inches deep. In the mountains between Highways Six and Seven, where the fearsome Monte Maggiore, all bristling with nests of enemy machine-guns, dominated the road to Rome, our soldiers had crawled up on hands and knees, clinging to the slippery rockface in fog and rain and in temperatures below freezing point dressed in ordinary battledress never meant for mountaineering in the depth of winter. Supplies had to be carried up by the men, as not even pack mules could negotiate the ascent. Even iron rations ran out, and in some cases it took a whole day to bring down the wounded, many of whom died on the long trek bumping down the mountainside. And all this was taking place under ferocious and non-stop enemy firing from above. Behind every rock, each crag, lurked a machine-gun and its crew, armed to the teeth and continually kept supplied by reinforcements brought up the northern, easier slopes.

Under the prevailing weather conditions and the deadly, thundering barrage from above, the fortitude of these two armies, Mark Clark's American Fifth and our own proud and intrepid Eighth, almost passes understanding. The Germans had to be picked out and dislodged one by one, in hand-to-hand fighting, and it was one of them or one of us, who tumbled over the edge each time. Names like Cassino, La Difensa, Venafro, Filignano, the Garigliano and the Sangro, bring back memories of fierce, dogged fighting, of unflinching valour and tenacity, and fearful, appalling casualties.

The bombing of the monastery at Cassino, which raised such furious controversy, was inevitably used by the enemy as powerful anti-Allied propaganda. Whether the building was used as an observation post or not is a point which has never really been established. It is however difficult to imagine the Germans not taking advantage of such

a position. The important fact to remember is that it domi
nated Highway Six, one of the three main roads to Rome
along which the army was to be launched, and when
it came to a choice between men and stones, General
Alexander always spared the men, even if venerable old
monuments had to bite the dust as a result.

Some of the troops had been in battle since the landings
at Salerno, but hungry, cold and weary though they were,
their unwavering steadfastness and their cheerfulness never
left them. This is a tale which ought to be told in novel
form by a contemporary Tolstoy. I can only report from
the clipped, brief bulletins and communiqués which
reached us well behind the lines, and from meeting some
of the men who came away on leave for a short spell before
returning to their man-made hell on the mountainside. It
is a wonder that so many retained their sanity. I met a shy
young British Army Major of nineteen at the time, who
had been promoted from Second-Lieutenant to his present
exalted rank in one day, by rising through the successive
stages as his superior officers were getting killed around
him.

When it became obvious to all that the Allies, once they
had broken through the Winter Line, were making steady
progress up the Leg, the Romans, taking heart, set up a
network of resistance under the command of the heroic
General Montezemola. For a time all was well, and useful
information about the enemy trickled through the lines
to the Allies. But the Germans, who had been watching
all along, set a trap for the poor general, into which he
fell. However, in spite of atrocious torture at the Chamber
of Horrors in the infamous Via Tasso, he never gave the
show away, nor breathed the name of a single one of his
colleagues.

In March 1944 the Communists, who never missed a
trick, and played an important though no doubt interested
part in the liberation of Italy, tacked themselves onto the

Resistance Movement in Rome, and set off a bomb as a squad of SS soldiers were marching past, blowing thirty-two of them into Eternity. In the reprisals, at the Ardeatini caves outside Rome, the General was one of the three hundred Italians who were machine-gunned, shovelled into the caves and walled up inside. When the Allies arrived in Rome, the mass grave was opened up, and Sandy MacKendrick, Head of Film Production of PWB, made a documentary of the event, through most of which I had to sit with my hands over my eyes.

The Ludovisi Hotel, the PWB Mess in Rome, was a dark, dingy and smelly dungeon. The musty little hall was the lair of a sour-faced porter who had no illusions left after occupation first by the SS, and then by the Allies. He took no trouble to disguise his contempt for humanity, and who could blame him under the circumstances?

'Come with me, signorina,' he ordered when I arrived, and letting me drag my kitbag along the corridor without help, he dumped me in the Mess office. A swarthy American sergeant looked up as I came in, then, ignoring my presence, started to chat with his mate. So, preparing for a long wait, I fished out my book, climbed on top of my kitbag and began to read.

'Whatya want, sis?' he asked after a while.

'I've been told to report here to work in Basic News. Can you give me a room, please?'

'Ha. A room. Ya hear that? The dame wants a room. You'll be lucky if you get a bed.'

Thinking I would be even luckier if I got a bed to myself, I said, 'A bed will do. I'm not fussy, as long as there are no bugs.'

'You find that out for yourself, sis, not my department. Go up to the second floor. Room 76.'

My new quarters would have been perfectly reasonable under different circumstances. A dark little lobby was shut off from the corridor by ill-fitting glass doors, and inside that domain was a grimy bathroom with the inevitable chipped linoleum on the floor, and next to it a really filthy loo, as only Italian loos can be when they try. Suddenly, as I was peering into the stinking hole, the chain, pulled by an invisible hand, came down and flushed out the bowl. In time, I was to become used to this particular feature of our convenience, but it was disconcerting not to be able to make it function when necessity demanded. The bedroom contained the inestimable luxury of twin beds, real spoiling that, as I was no longer used to a whole bed to myself. As the room seemed unoccupied, I chose the bed nearest the window. Two floors below, the street was teeming with Italians shouting at one another, and assorted soldiery coming and going. GIs, as was their wont, sat on the pavement opposite, smoking, chewing gum, hailing the signorinas, and generally passing the time of day.

That evening, as so often happened, there was a power-cut. Looking around the dim twilight of the dining-room, I couldn't see a face I knew. 'Ah well, starting again from scratch,' I thought to myself, opening *War and Peace* on the table beside my plate.

Opposite the hotel were town steps leading into the Via Veneto, at the bottom of which stood the PWB offices. These had also been occupied by the SS, who had obviously done themselves proud, for behind every major office were marble floor bedrooms and luxurious bathrooms.

Rumour had it that our Black Propaganda, which was usually lodged apart in select, exclusive quarters, had settled down with us in the Ludovisi this time. Many of them, who seemed to enjoy the surroundings, spent quite a lot of time in the bar, surrounded by an admiring crowd avid for stories of their exploits. There was one particularly flamboyant Colonel who kept us all spellbound with tales of his adventures behind the lines. One of his turns was taking potshots at the fig leaves of the statues in the little piazzas with his revolver, to demonstrate the infallible accuracy of his firing at long range with small arms. The Roman citizenry, gathered in the summer twilight, were as riveted by the performance as we were.

Major Twist, in charge of Admin as usual, instructed me to find my way to Basic News, which was tucked up in the Via Moretto, about a mile away from the Mess. And how, I asked, was I to get there? Was there any official transport? And what about returning from the night shift alone through the fearful streets of Rome at two o'clock in the morning? Major Twist, who was evasive about this, made it plain that he was not interested in my transport problems. I might approach the Americans about it, he suggested, as Basic News was, once more, an almost entirely US operation, with me as the only Limey on the newsdesk. The Editor, when I asked him, answered curtly, 'Find your own transport, honey, that's your problem.' And promptly put me down for the night shift as I was, once again, the youngest member of the office.

Eventually the question resolved itself in two ways, both as unattractive as each other, so I laid them on in turns. The only other reporter on the desk who was not American was a tough little South African terrier of a man with square yellow teeth (fake, as I was soon to find out), a really filthy temper, and a bottle of Scotch permanently at his elbow beside his typewriter. The greatest phobia of his life was coloured people, or bloody niggers, as he called them.

Sometimes, when my heart failed me at the thought of the long walk back to the Mess among the footpads, the murderers and the rapists of the night, I firmly seized Scottie, my South African colleague, by the arm and steered him off in the direction of the Ludovisi. Even plastered as he was, it was a comfort to have him, at least when he was able to stand up. But the fresh air often knocked him out altogether, so that I had half to carry and half to drag him all the way up the hill to the hotel. From time to time, as we passed an American requisitioned hotel, or Mess, or PX on the way, with a coloured military policeman on guard on the door, up tottered my friend unsteadily to his feet, revived by what he called the filthy pong of the bloody bastard, and punched the astonished soldier in the nose. Reaction was swift and deadly. A huge black fist would flash forward, smashing my companion's face into next week, sending his false teeth flying into the gutter, while the gigantic darkie rumbled, 'You'd better get your boyfriend home quick, mam, unless you want to spend the night in the cooler with him.'

And apologising miserably while grovelling in the gutter for the teeth, I would shoulder my irascible burden again, and stagger along the street once more, until we reached the next coloured MP guarding the next doorstep, and the whole performance was re-enacted from beginning to end. After a couple of nights of these antics, I usually decided to face the perils of the street alone. The people out on the prowl at that hour were inevitably up to no good. Apart from the usual run of professional criminals, there was a terrifying gang of juvenile brigands armed to the teeth with stolen bayonets, who knifed you in the back first, and searched you afterwards for money and valuables. You were not even safe on a bicycle, as they would charge that like a pack of wild dogs, promptly despatch the rider, and make off with the bike.

When I decided to set off alone, I walked in the middle of the road with hatpin at the ready, plunging it without qualms into anybody who made a grab at me. Even now, I feel no guilt whatever at the thought of perhaps having badly wounded one or two of these unattractive characters. They certainly staggered back under the thrust with gratifying squeals of outraged agony.

That first liberated summer in Rome was very hot. Long rivulets of sweat poured down the faces of the buildings in the narrow back streets which I loved to explore. As usual, night duty meant lovely long days to myself, which I couldn't bear to waste in sleep. My habit of quick catnaps when nothing of special interest was going on made up for that. Those glorious free days were spent climbing about the Colosseum, which was overgrown with vegetation and comfortably chaotic inside.

The Forum opposite, a wilderness of weeds and wild flowers, was crawling with adders, caterpillars, and all kinds of extraordinary Italian bugs and beetles. There was one particular kind, curiously shaped like a little partridge which, unable to hold up the weight of its corpulent body, shuffled around on permanently bended knees. I sat for hours among the ruins in the sun, busily sketching piles of ancient stones and pillars, gracefully draped with ivy, convolvulus and wild woodbine, or just staring about, perfectly happy, watching the lizards and the butterflies.

All round the haven of this little nature reserve roared the life of the Eternal City, with thousands of military vehicles of every shape and kind, and three-wheeled camionetta taxis running on two-stroke motorcycle engines, the only kind of motorised transport available to the civilian population at the time.

On other occasions I trekked all the way out to the Via Appia Antica, spending long hours dabbling away with a paintbrush at water colours of the ruins lining the road. Then, squatting under an umbrella pine, I gobbled my sandwiches before setting off again along the road to Rome, past the Quo Vadis chapel where Saint Peter's fate was sealed, heading for another long hot night of work in Basic News.

Sometimes on Sundays we drove out to Ostia at the mouth of the Tiber, but this war-scarred area and still-mined beaches held little charm. Lake Brancaccio was a far more attractive bathing spot, well away from blown bridges and crumpled villages. Villa d'Este at Tivoli, with its abandoned terraces and in spite of its stilled fountains, was a joy to walk about in, undisturbed by the fussing of keepers and the gawping of tourists. Wild life, unperturbed by the to-ing and fro-ing of armies, had taken possession of the grounds, and the buzzing and droning of bees and beetles, and the shrill sound of the cicadas, all triumphant at having won *their* battle against their age-old enemy the gardeners, was music to my ears.

In the warm evenings when not on night duty, and if I could persuade someone to come along as bodyguard, I loved to walk in the Borghese and the Pincio gardens in Rome, under the mulberry trees where tiny silkworms, dangling on their threads in their thousands, wove live hair-nets around your head. It would have been lovely to row on the Tiber, but the swiftness of its rushing waters made boating impossible. The Castel San Angelo on its banks, being permanently closed, was another of my frustrations, as I never managed to get inside, where Benvenuto Cellini spent so many years of his life as a prisoner, spitting out his rotten teeth and having ecstatic visions of Truth and Light.

Saint Peter's came into its own on Christmas night, when the Pope celebrated mass at midnight before a congregation of forty thousand people crammed shoulder to shoulder, and numbering as many Allied soldiers as honest Roman citizens. The sound of all those voices singing together, rolling and echoing round the roof, was an awesome experience. At the end of the service the Pope was carried round the cathedral on his throne on the powerful shoulders of the Swiss Guard, after which we walked all the way back to the Mess, in the snow, under the hard, cold stars of the fifth and last Christmas of the war.

In spite of all this painting and sketching out of doors, I still felt that I was getting nowhere. A convincing way of putting down on paper the wonder and the splendour of it all eluded me altogether. So deciding to take the bull by the horns, I marched into an art gallery on the Via Veneto, and asked the man in charge if one of his artists could be persuaded to give me a few lessons.

Apart from crime, one thing which never flagged in Rome was the art world. Constant exhibitions were going up on the walls of the numerous galleries and the artists, bolstering one another's morale, continued to paint on a near-starvation diet, all living together in the enchanting little Via Margutta, which looked rather like a well-kept London mews. Window-boxes perched on every ledge, and flower baskets hung from arches and porticoes. The doors were painted in bright cheerful colours, and the studios were a revelation of artistic design, a subtle mixture of antique and modern furniture, and everywhere reigned the most riotous and unconventional combinations of colour.

Here, the essence of the Italian soul, generous and optimistic if given half a chance, had kept itself going, untainted by all the disappointments, bitterness and corruption of defeat. The joyful spontaneity and effervescent creativeness of this little community formed an oasis of sanity and hope in the heart of the violent, rapacious and crime-infested city. It was an immeasurable privilege to be introduced to it. Giuseppe Capogrossi, my painting master, had a working studio in another part of the town, which was stifling hot in summer and a vast refrigerator in winter. I felt dreadfully sorry for the poor purple-skinned model, aptly named Violetta, who always posed in the nude, whatever the weather. She had an American boyfriend somewhere along the line to the front, of whom she had had no news for several weeks. The story was pitifully familiar. Signorinas were picked up by the soldiers here, there and everywhere, and then dropped and promptly forgotten as soon as another took her place. All perfectly normal wartime procedure, but how to explain this to

Violetta? Undertaking to track down the missing GI, and nosing around for information, I was suddenly summoned by the ever-watchful Major Twist, who ordered me very curtly to drop all this interfering at once. Anglo-American relations were always at the top of everybody's mind, Priority Number One, which if not handled with the greatest circumspection, could endanger the entire outcome of the war. And although a split would have meant total disaster to the Allies, it was ludicrous to exaggerate the effect of my efforts to that extent.

'Il faut toujours chercher la ligne,' Signor Capogrossi used to say over and over again, encouraging my fumbling efforts and finding more virtue in some hopeless mess than in what I considered a more dashing effort. Patient, tolerant and forbearing, he loved England and, having obviously never seen a smog, what he called her gentle mists, and soft landscapes. So much Italian sun and harsh contrast was too violent for his nature. Recently I was delighted to find some of his sensitive etchings in a London art gallery.

By the end of August, General Alexander was ready to attack the Gothic Line, the last stronghold in Italy which frustrated our advance into the Po Valley. Bristling with formidable fortifications in depth, made up of tank traps, turrets, concrete pill-boxes and almost every inch of the ground planted with mines, it stretched from Spezia in the West to the Adriatic coast.

The Allied Commander, General Alexander, who had recently lost seven divisions for the benefit of the South of France landings, was now to have the French Expeditionary Force snaffled away from him as well. He wrote in desperation, 'The ghost of Anvil [he obviously hadn't caught up with Dragoon] hangs heavy over the battle front ... Armies have a very delicate sense, and they are beginning to look over their shoulders. You will no doubt remember the Biblical quotation, "If the trumpet give an uncertain sound, who shall prepare himself for battle?"'

But Churchill, unusually brutal with his favourite general, and no doubt under unbearable pressure from Roosevelt himself, emphatically confirmed Alexander's orders to wipe out the German forces in the shortest possible time, and with whatever forces available, thereby bringing the war in Italy to an end *as soon as possible*. To say the least, Alex was being sorely tried! But true to his own patient self, he soldiered on without protest.

The original plan of bearding the Gothic Line in the West had to be changed, as General Oliver Leese, who was in charge of the operation since Monty had been switched to the Western front, preferred to launch the attack on the Adriatic coast. With astute manoeuvring and careful planning, he managed to get his troops over the mountains undetected. Kesselring, the German General, who had been expecting the breakthrough in the West, had to bundle his forces over to the other side with all possible speed. As soon as Alexander realised this, he ordered Mark Clark to press on through the Giogo and Futa passes, thus carrying out the original strategy after all.

Had the Allied armies been standing at full strength, victory would have been swift and final. As it was our depleted forces suffered heavy casualties, and were prevented by their diminished numbers from storming the Gothic Line there and then. The winter rains, deciding on an early start, came down in buckets, and for the second year running the troops had to confront the now familiar swilling mud of another Italian winter.

Unbelievable though it may sound, Alex was to lose five more divisions to the Western front before his own offensive the following spring. When Churchill implacably told him to carry out whatever orders were assigned to him with any material remaining at his disposal, he meekly replied, 'You already know that my only wish is to serve

[122]

where I am most useful, and feeling that way, I am well content.' This is the only time I ever felt impatient with my hero. I wanted to shake him. In the face of the enemy he was a man, or rather, a superman. Why did he have to be a mouse to Churchill, whose bullying nature would drive and pressurise and take advantage until he met resistance? And this he would never get from Alexander who would let himself be walked over and trampled on without a squeak. It made my blood boil.

The last battle which was to finish off the Germans in Italy was launched on 9 April, 1945, and was 'as hard fought as the first', in Alexander's own words. It resulted from a combination of enormously competent and minutely synchronised bombardments and artillery fire, and was set up with a cunning use of double-bluff, making it as obvious as possible that we were attacking in the West, so that the Germans would assume this to be a trick, and rush off to the Venetian coast on the other side, which they obligingly did. While all the time the big offensive *was* coming from the West after all. Like the Romans before them, so often fooled by Hannibal with similar tricks and equal success, the Germans, whenever they tried to be subtle, invariably fell into the trap.

7

BASIC NEWS in Rome was conducted by an Irishman from New York. You never knew why or when he would explode, and his rages were like the wrath of God. We didn't get on and he enjoyed tormenting me by chopping Churchill's speeches which annoyed and upset me. Without giving any reasons, I asked for a transfer to Greece. The Big Boss was perfectly charming, and promised to remember me as soon as a vacancy occurred, but at the present moment, Athens was in a state of rebellion (as if *that* would put anyone off) and no women were allowed into Greece at all. So, for the time being, I had no choice but to stick it out.

I was also unlucky, to say the least, that my bedroom in the Mess happened to be exactly below that of two officers who would stagger up to bed just as I had dropped off to sleep, holding each other up, and by the time they reached their room, some fearsome argument had usually broken out between them. Fisticuffs inevitably followed, and soon they were hurling army boots, tin hats and empty bottles at each other, until one of them mercifully passed out. Up to that blessed moment, the ceiling above my head shook and rattled as I lay in bed, clutching my bear for comfort, as plaster flaked down over my face. Occasionally they mistook the floor, and tried to force an entry into my bedroom. As there were no locks, it was child's play to get in, and once installed, they were delighted with their mistake, and showed no desire to regain their own quarters. Several times I had to push, carry and drag them out, dropping them in the corridor where they passed out, while I feverishly barricaded myself in by trundling a bed against the glass doors of the lobby.

One night I came up to find Joy Packer in the empty bed. From that moment on life looked up with a wave of light-hearted gaiety. Her sophistication, and her sense of humour brought back the realisation that somewhere sanity and a civilised way of life still existed. So that through the magic of her wit, the loo which flushed itself whenever the spirit moved it, the bouncing boots on the floor above, the drunks lurching about in the Mess downstairs, and the constant freezing cold of that winter, became a steady source of private jokes and endless amusement. She, the well named, was certainly a great joy to have around. In her modesty, she never let on that she was a well-known writer, and the wife of the Naval C-in-C's Chief of Staff at Caserta. This all trickled through later, a crumb at a time. One day her book arrived from the publishers, and then she had to come clean. As the story of her life, following her husband's ship around the world, more often than not as a working journalist herself, it was fascinating and I couldn't put it down. But even then I didn't realise that she was busily writing us all up for her next book.

On one occasion, when she and I were lying in bed in the dark, chatting of this and that, we heard the dreaded pair approach the lobby doors.

'Cooee, girls, here we come,' warbled the English Captain in drunken tones. Leaping out of bed, I hissed through my teeth, 'I'll deal with them.'

Joy, awaiting developments and storing it all up for the next instalment, lay there in bed without a word. Outside our window, and hanging on an enormous iron hook, was a huge barometer five foot high and at least two wide. Leaning out of the window, and with a sudden upsurge of strength which I didn't know I possessed, I hauled this up into the room, dragged it across the floor, and propped it up under the handle of the glass door. This ramrod, I thought, would provide invincible protection. And although our would-be visitors were lurching and stumbling about with a fearful clatter, I told them quite calmly to buzz off, without the customary note of panic in my voice, to which they were by now accustomed.

So, hearing none of the usual shrill and piercing screams with which I normally greeted them ('Scram, you bloody bastards', and worse), they obviously took this lack of insult as an invitation, and crashed heavily into the glass doors, which burst inwards, sending the barometer spinning across the lobby to explode like a blockbuster on the opposite wall. Glass splinters flew in all directions, spewing rivers of mercury, which gushed and flowed merrily all over the floor. Anyone would think that an experience of this kind might have acted as a deterrent to our nocturnal visitors. True, one of the officers retired to his drying-out establishment for another spell, but the English Captain became more assiduous than ever. To avoid him downstairs, when he was standing on a table in the bar haranguing the delighted denizens of the Mess with flamboyant patriotic speeches, I would creep up to bed early and settle down cosily with *War and Peace* and my bear, and when I was lucky, a bar of NAAFI chocolate as well. But in no time at all he was there, sitting on the end of my bed, with Joy, student of human nature, watching the proceedings.

'Why do you hate me so much?' he asked peevishly.

'Don't be an ass. I don't hate you at all. I just hate people getting drunk, that's all.'

'It's not only that. I know you don't like me. You just don't care. And not just for me. You don't care for anyone. You've just got a bloody great stone for a heart.'

Oh God, I thought, here we go. 'Don't be a fool,' I said impatiently. 'Do you think I would hang around bored to death at your ghastly parties, to bring you home when you are all plastered to the eyebrows, just to save you from the Military Police, if I didn't care?'

'Oh,' he said, 'that's not the kind of care I mean. That's just bloody governess kind of care!'

'Well, it's the only one you're going to get. And to begin with, you can get off my feet.' And I gave him a whacking great kick under the bedclothes. His mouth fell open, his eyes popped, his moustache stuck out in horizontal spikes, and he got up and left the room in an elaborate tip-toeing kind of step, like a stork picking his way through a brood of eggs, and I had to dive under the bedclothes so that he wouldn't see me laugh, while from Joy's bed came a discreet little giggle.

One evening as I was quietly dining at the Nirvanetta Club with a nice young Subaltern on leave from the Gothic Line, and we were enjoying a relaxed chat about nothing in particular, both minding our own business, a large bulky figure suddenly loomed over me. My arm was grabbed, and I was roughly hoisted out of my chair. Speechless with horror, I found myself face to face with the infamous Major from Algiers.

'Don't look so pleased to see me,' he said sourly. 'And don't just stand there like a tombstone. Get moving.' And he shoved me along to the dance floor.

'You've improved,' he remarked presently, 'but don't take that as a compliment. It just means that you're growing up, and your eyes have narrowed. You'll do for me now.' Too agitated for speech, I tried to wriggle away, but he squashed me up against his chest in a vice-like grip.

'None of your tricks this time, my girl,' he snapped. 'You're not getting away, so don't try anything on, or you'll be sorry.' And he brought his hard mouth down on to mine, and his tongue squeezed in between my lips like a huge slimy slug. His moustache, crammed into my nostrils, stifled me so that, in a blind panic, I brought my teeth together with all the strength of my jaw muscles, and scrunched them hard into the revolting lump in my mouth. As he staggered back with a roar of pain, I punched him hard in the wind for good measure, then fled back to my table, where my young officer was regarding the proceedings with a mildly astonished eye.

'Let's get out of here,' I hissed, handing him his hat.

'Whatever for? It's only nine o'clock.'

'Come on, for God's sake, I've bitten the Major.'

'You've *what*?'

'His mouth is full of blood. He'll kill me.' And ducking between the dancers and keeping a low profile, I scuttled away towards the door as fast as I could.

'He won't come after you now, don't worry,' panted the Lieutenant, trying to catch up with me as I was travelling up the Via Veneto at a smartish pace.

'You don't know him, you just don't know him,' I said with a shudder.

'What *you* don't know, my dear, is that you could get him court-martialled for this. And *he* knows it. Don't worry, he won't bother you any more now. He's probably learnt his lesson.'

Which was quite true, for never again did I see or hear from that Major. But I couldn't help saying regretfully, 'He got off lightly. I could have used my hatpin.' But there hadn't been time for that.

Norman, who was a poet, had been, like so many of his colleagues, a member of J. Walter Thompson until joining the German leaflet section of PWB. The prose he produced now was destined to be dropped by the light bombers of Tactical Air Force on German troops, and to supplement the leaflets produced by the Advance PWB Units attached to the Fifth and Eighth Armies. Captain Beauclerk, who was in charge of PWB Eighth Army, had his own prickly bunch of writers whose task it was to address the enemy front lines immediately ahead. The keystone of this operation was Front Post, a weekly news sheet giving the German soldiers the latest news of Allied bombing of their homeland, and any little bit of bad news (from the enemy's point of view) about spectacular advances on the Western and Eastern fronts. 'Don't get yourselves killed so far from home when you will be needed to reconstruct your own country before long,' was one of the encouraging messages of this little newspaper. All of which was shot over the lines by our artillery at the front, tucked up inside smoke shells.

From Bari on the Adriatic coast originated the strategic leaflets entrusted to the big long-range bombers which went much further afield, right into the heart of Austria. And between the two sections, Tactical and Strategic, continual rivalry existed, each wanting to swallow up the other, seeing no reason for the necessity of more than one section.

A great brain and one of the few sane members of PWB, when he had nothing better to do, Norman would grab me by the hand as he passed, saying, 'Come on, let's go out to dinner.' And off we'd go to the Nirvanetta. Halfway through the meal, after he had downed several bottles of Chianti, he would scramble to his feet, muttering "Fraid I'm a bit drunk. Must go and sleep it off. You stay here. I'll be back.'

And I would finish my dinner, order one or two sticky liqueurs, known as Strega, with the coffee, and if it was summer, watch the dancers gyrating under the stars. The smell of syringa and jasmine lay heavy on the air, and it was all very pleasant and peaceful, and I had no trouble in forgetting all about the war and Basic News for a couple of hours.

In winter, we sat indoors, and Gaby, the refugee Hungarian dancer, would give us more than our ration of cabaret, to pass the time. Between her caperings, everybody clamoured for her to join their table. Very young (she said she was sixteen), her vitality and ebullience made her great fun, although there was no way of communicating with her unless you could speak Hungarian or Italian. By then we could all get by tolerably well in Italian, except for the older officers from the First World War, who simply stuck an O onto the end of English words, then roared imprecations at the puzzled faces of the 'Wops' they were addressing.

Two or three hours later Norman would reappear, and we would resume our jerky shuffling around the dance floor. Sometimes he took me to visit an Italian opera singer who had a warm and cosy flat at the top of the Spanish Steps. 'A sensible woman,' was how Norman described her. 'She was nice to the Germans, and now she is nice to us, so she is always comfortable, with plenty of fuel and all the food she wants.' This shocked me to the core at first. I didn't understand how he could admire such treachery. 'Don't be so bourgeois,' he admonished. 'She is sophisticated enough to understand that war has nothing to do with women.'

All very well, I thought, but it seems to have quite a bit to do with me, in one way and another. I must say that she was always very welcoming and her cynicism sparkled with a very engaging brand of cheerfulness. Picking up her guitar, all hung with gaily coloured ribbons, she would start singing as soon as Norman had poured out the contents of the bottle he had brought. I remember one particularly jolly ditty which started with, 'E venuto l'Ambasciatore, col plume sul capello,' and in a few minutes we were all joining in. But however much I enjoyed it, the thought of Germans singing and laughing with her as we were now doing ourselves, just a few months before, nagged away at my tight little priggish and unsophisticated mind.

More often than not, when I got back to the Ludovisi for dinner, the place was almost in total darkness owing to a power cut. One candle flickered in the draughts of the hall, and another stood on the counter of the little bar. The new Mess Officer who was my old friend from the Cornouailles, and Norman, often appeared from the office bearing one more candle and a chessboard between them. It was always a pleasure to watch them play. There was something very comforting and secure in the sight of an ordinary game of chess being played by candlelight in such surroundings. These two were the only ones ever to indulge in the game. There we were in the midst of wartime Rome in the dark of a power cut, with every kind of crime, vice, murder, and treachery rampaging about the streets, while a few miles up north, young men were staggering about in the slithery, shifting mud of the Italian winter, screwing up their courage to lead their patrols into the trip-wires and booby traps of no-man's land. And the ability which the Loot and Norman had of detaching themselves from all this, and becoming utterly absorbed in their game, generated a kind of serenity which was very soothing to the spirit. So I always lurked in their vicinity, absorbing this rare quality through every pore, either dozing in a chair, or slumped on a step, or crouching under the grand piano in the so-called lounge, or wherever they happened to settle with their game. Quite inured to my presence, they took not the slightest notice of me, so that I was able to relax, feeling as contented and undisturbed as the flies on the wall.

That winter we were all very cold, and the food, though

adequate, was dismally dull. Spam, waffles and maple syrup for almost every meal. We were used to that, but when after Christmas it became scarce as well, and we had to go onto iron rations, many of my colleagues became vociferous in their complaints. The reason was, as I knew from writing up the copy, that almost an entire convoy bringing supplies to the Med had bitten the dust of the Deep. This meant of course that a pitiful number of sailors would have gone down, while the survivors were machine-gunned in the water from the air. But these were matters which couldn't be mentioned to the grumblers, on pain of being labelled a creeping Jesus, a goody-goody or a godawful do-gooder. So it was better to keep your mouth shut and chew your iron rations in silence.

Rome doesn't often see snow, but in 1944 there were some heavy falls around Christmas and the New Year, and for several days the fountains in the piazzas were frozen into fantastic stalactites of ice. We went into the Apennines with toboggans in the back of the PU, and spent a couple of Sundays rattling down the slopes where only a year before the army had so desperately fought for every inch of the ground, and Monty, along the East coast, had at last to fight hard for his laurels, taking ten days to cross the Sangro River with heavy casualties, as the German General Kesselring had somehow managed to spirit his forces through the filthy weather of the mountains undetected.

By November the year before, both the Fifth and the Eighth Armies were firmly stuck in the mud of the Winter Line on the south side of the Abruzzi mountains, and once more true heroism had shown its glowing face. Troops were continually being withdrawn from General Alexander's forces, to be re-equipped and re-formed for the Western Front, and the soldiers couldn't help feeling that they were no longer top priority in the minds of the politicians conducting the war. In spite of this discouraging discovery, the men hammered on with undiminished tenacity, while a great reshuffle of the pack of cards was taking place at the top. Overlord had to be equipped with able, as well as popular commanders. General Sir Henry Maitland Wilson (Jumbo to the troops) became Supreme Commander in the Mediterranean, while Eisenhower, much against his will, remained saddled with the irrepressible Monty, at which an audible sigh of relief had been heard the length and breadth of Italy, YES, in spite of the Enfant Terrible's personal popularity with his own troops.

General Oliver Leese had taken command of the Eighth, and our dearly-beloved Alex retained command of Allied Armies in Italy. He and Mark Clark got on well, mostly on account of Alex's unceasing and patient efforts in that direction. And this in spite of major provocation when, ignoring orders, General Clark marched into Rome, instead of pursuing and annihilating the German army east of the capital, according to his instructions. But the temptation to be first to enter Rome from the South since Belisarius fourteen hundred years before, had been too great to resist. And nobody, Alex least of all, held it against him. Moreover, it was thought that the liberation of Rome by US troops would give America's morale a tremendous boost, making her feel that perhaps she wasn't altogether wasting her substance in Italy after all, which in American eyes was only desirable for the capture of Rome as a kind of world coup in a gigantic promotion campaign. All politics again.

Mark Clark considered that his men deserved this prize after the terrible beating they had taken at Anzio, one of the bloodiest attempts of the war at breaching the soft underbelly of Europe. Only thirty miles south of the capital, the object of these landings had been to thrust up towards the Alban Hills and capture the city before the Germans, taken by surprise, had a chance of defending their rear. If immediate advantage had been taken of the good weather and lack of opposition, this aim might have been achieved. Unfortunately the General in charge, feeling that his troops might be cut off from their base and encircled by the enemy, refused to budge, thereby turning the beachhead into one of the most disastrous Anglo-American graveyards of the war. The Germans, realising the situation, brought heavy reinforcements, and fiercely defended the position. So much so that the Allied troops were tottering on the brink of withdrawal when General Alexander, mercifully arriving on the scene, promptly raised morale all round, relieved the broken commander of his duties and installed US General Truscott in his place. From then on, against overwhelming odds, the indomitable courage of the troops, fighting with a new fury to make up for the bungling of their leader, turned the tide of battle and carried the day.

But in spite of all this, and against the will of the Generals, the Americans still withdrew another seven of their divisions to add to the South of France invasion. Poor Alexander, probably feeling desperately worried, but uttering no word of complaint, was struck down with jaundice. I met him only once towards the end of the campaign, by which time he had become a Field-Marshal, and Supreme Commander. The famous charm, of which everybody who met him spoke, enveloped me like an invisible net and froze me to the spot, unable to open my mouth. But what could the tiddler from Basic News possibly have to say to the Field-Marshal anyway? He smiled, said a few words which, owing to my agitation, were lost on me, and walked away.

None of the other Commanders I met glowed with the same aura. Lord Tedder, Commander-in-Chief of the Royal Air Force, who often invited us to cocktail parties at his villa in Algiers, was courteous and approachable, in a perfectly charming and ordinary way; General Oliver Leese, who received the guests at a Charity Ball with me in London, was jolly and easy-going, and Admiral Cunningham, Naval Commander-in-Chief, sharp and witty and never missing a trick, was gracious enough to allow me to join a minesweeping expedition in the Adriatic. General Eisenhower, to my regret, I never met personally.

Considering what a refined and fastidious personage Lady Packer was, she took the prevailing squalor of PWB very much in her stride, but when Jan, arriving from Algiers, was found by her one fine evening parked in our minute lobby on an army cot, she was truly shocked. 'But there's no air, and the loo flushes all through the night,' she exclaimed indignantly. Jan and I, used to roughing it, only laughed. We were glad to see each other again, and where she slept was immaterial to her. Joy said no more at the time, but remembering the set of her mouth, I suspected her of descending on the office and sorting out the Mess Sergeant, with whom she frequently battled on behalf of her friends. Anyway, in a very short time, Jan was given a room of her own, which she effectively transformed within minutes of occupation by simply shifting the furniture around and spreading some of her expensive belongings about the place.

The Christmas period of that icy winter was brightened by a series of various jollifications which made up for the slush of the streets and the piercing cold which kept us permanently shivering in our inadequate clothing and unheated premises. Christmas Eve was spent at the Union Jack Mess, where Fleet Street men of renown, headed by Lord (then Hugh to us) Cudlipp, produced an English newspaper for the Services. Presiding at the party in person, the Editor made the punch himself, adding extra little touches throughout the evening. I remember thinking that he looked like Mephistopheles with his jet-black hair and eyebrows, and his curvy, mobile mouth, and the fantastic energy which kept him leaping non-stop around the punch-bowl with a bottle in each hand. All this activity continued unabated until I left for Midnight Mass at Saint Peter's.

On Christmas day, I lunched with some of them in the sunshine on the terrace of the Pincio Officers' Club, where we imbibed vast quantities of Christ's Tears, a sweet and sticky wine called Lachrimae Christi, and on New Year's eve, there was a dance at the Ambassadors Hotel to which several of us went in a great jolly crowd. Jan unfortunately had to sit apart, as she was currently being hotly pursued by a well-bred and elegant young man in the shape of a Loot who knew her family in Boston, and was determined to marry her there and then, war or no war. 'He's got absolutely everything going for him,' she would say miserably, unable to make up her mind.

'Isn't there *anything* he is a bit short of?' I enquired hopefully.

'Well, he's not ... wildly exciting ...'

'You mean he's deadly dull, and let's face it, you're not in love with him.'

Looking even more dejected, she heaved a great sigh. 'I ought to be, he's really too good for me.'

'When in doubt, do nothing,' I said from the depth of my own experience. 'Remember that when you are married, he will expect to be around quite a bit. Men can be awfully possessive. Could you bear that?'

Joy, whose experience was even wider, asked more succinctly, 'Could you bear to go to bed with him?'

As I hadn't properly cottoned on to that aspect of marriage yet, the argument didn't mean much to me, but since Jan made no reply, and I longed to appear to be in the know, I chipped in, 'How can she tell until she's tried?' at which they both laughed, never doubting that I knew what I was talking about.

Next day the young man must have been sent packing, because Jan joined us at a very merry New Year's lunch at the Officers' club, where one of my Fleet Street chums kept us in fits throughout the meal with stories of his pre-war adventures on the *Daily Express*, and Joy told us tales of life in Cape Town when she was a child. Jan and I, delighted to be entertained, found it unnecessary to contribute yarns of our own.

There were also cocktail and dinner parties at the Embassy, at which you always met new faces, since people were continually coming and going between the Balkans, Greece, Egypt, England and the United States. Another favourite pastime was what we called swanning, a delightful form of gadding about and seeing the world by hitching lifts in military vehicles and aircraft, which the authorities made a half-hearted attempt to discourage.

Among our American civilians was a young man named Kurt Vorak, very clever, and Professor of Philosophy at one of the major American universities when he was not doing his bit for the war. He had dreamy, protruding pink-rimmed eyes, permanently inflamed nostrils and a long thin neck with an enormous Adam's apple which gambolled up and down his windpipe whenever he spoke or swallowed. Utterly mesmerised by this remarkable phenomenon, I couldn't help staring every time he sat opposite me in the dining-room, until one day, perhaps misunderstanding my interest, he invited me to go to a concert with him. As I could never find anyone else to come with me, I accepted with alacrity. So off we trotted to Radio Roma, where a number of tickets were always reserved for the Allies. Halfway through the programme the conductor, who had been working himself into a frenzy, suddenly went rigid and toppled face forward into the orchestra. A great roar of appreciation rose from the audience, who stampeded in their enthusiasm, all rushing forward to touch the Maestro as he was being carried out by the double bass and the first violin.

For me this was the beginning of a new Life of Culture.

We went to the opera, which was always first-class, and to the ballet, which wasn't, we visited all the churches, even the dull ones, all very systematically, after which we repaired to Kurt's digs for nuts and honey. This we consumed in a dark and smelly little dining-room lit by one candle in a far corner of the room. He lived in a murky little pension somewhere in a back street, where among the various discomforts he endured with stoic resignation were fearful cold, total lack of hot water, and of course no electric light. Anything, he used to say, to get away from the PWB rabble. Sometimes he took me to see Leonor Fini, the artist, in her luxurious studio, which she shared with a distinguished-looking Marchese who had abandoned his career in 'the Diplomatic' to follow his Muse on her advice. There wasn't much to be seen in his pictures, as he painted little white people trotting across a white canvas. But there were some fascinating parties, at which everybody was clever and sophisticated in a way which I could only dimly sense. A curious smell of incense (or was it pot?) pervaded the air, and they all talked in innuendoes. I knew I was on the edge of a world which I could not possibly penetrate, although I longed to do so. When I asked what it was all about, they laughed in a kindly, patronising way, but offered no explanation.

One fine, or rather, gloomy day, Joy was taken ill and whisked off to hospital, after which her Admiral spirited her away to Naples to recover. She was mad about her husband, who wrote her the most touching love letters, which she sometimes showed me, extolling the bliss and blessings of marriage. But I remained sceptical. Not all marriages, I was quite certain, were as happy as hers, which was quite an exceptional affair altogether.

That winter, Clare Booth Luce, who was doing a swoop around Europe with a bunch of Congressmen, landed in Rome with her entourage, and Joy saw a good deal of her, but I, at my small-fry level I missed the treat altogether.

Gradually the weather improved and spring was just round the corner, when suddenly, to my chagrin, Joy announced that she was moving north with her section. The South Africans, known as the Springboks, together with the New Zealanders and the Guards Brigade, took Florence, which the Germans had offered to declare an open city. In spite of fierce street-to-street fighting, destruction was limited to the blowing up by the enemy of all the bridges, except for the Ponte Vecchio. This relic of the Renaissance, a much smaller version of London Bridge, with shops strung along both sides from shore to shore, had been blocked off at both ends by the simple expedient of dynamiting the surrounding houses. Apart from that there was little damage, and the advance units of PWB were able to move in immediately. Joy and her pamphlets and photographs were urgently needed to follow up the successes of the Allied armies, so off she and her colleagues went one fine morning, packed into the back of a three-tonner. It was the first time I had seen her in battledress, and she looked very businesslike. Her departure left a gloomy gap, and the bedroom suddenly looked more drab and shabby than ever before. Once more on my own, I was quite glad to have a little point two-two revolver, which an English Major brought me back from Cairo. With this tucked up under my pillow, and hugging my bear like a hot-water bottle, I felt as safe as houses. But in the street at night on the way back from Basic News, I still preferred the hatpin. It was unexpected, quiet, and above all, deadly.

On 23 April, the British and the South Africans, having broken through the Gothic Line at last, met behind the German front at a little town surprisingly called Finale on the River Po, trapping a vast number of enemy troops in a circle of Allied fire and steel. And the Germans, realising the end had come, laid down their arms at 6 pm on 2 May, 1945—and the war in Italy was over.

There was a great party in the Ludovisi, and I alas, enjoyed myself a little too much, only getting to bed at four o'clock. When I woke up, my precious little revolver was gone, snatched away from under my head while I was fast asleep.

8

THE PSYCHOLOGICAL WARFARE Branch in Rome was
folding up, as all its multitudinous objectives were now
accomplished. This time, on reporting to what was left of
the Admin Department for instructions, the main body
having migrated to Florence, I was told to find my way
to Venice, the locale of my next job. No name, no address
was provided. PWB News Section, Venice, was all I had
to go by.

Well used to finding my way around by now the
hundreds of military and air force units, depots, airfields,
bombed-out towns and non-existent streets, I took this in
my stride. The first thing to do on arriving at a newly
liberated place was to call on the Town Major, and make
friends with him. He would always fit you in somewhere
for the night, fix you up with a tin of bully or a slab of
chocolate if no other meal was available, and he always
knew when and where the next army convoy was leaving from; there was always room for one more body on
a convoy.

In Florence I was in luck, as I was able to spend the night
in the PWB Mess there. Apart from the crumpled, dusty
banks of the river, there was little damage to be seen.

Before dinner I had time for an hour's canoeing down the main stream of the Arno, while children scampered about on the sandbanks between the rivulets, into which the ruins of the Ponte Trinità had collapsed in heaps of rubble. In the light of the setting sun I walked through the town, where snipers and machine-gun bullets pock-marked the severe countenance of the noble Renaissance palaces, standing otherwise undamaged in their solemn piazzas and narrow medieval streets.

Early the next morning I climbed into the courier to Bologna. All courier drivers were surely powered by the same urges. This one was different from his Naples colleague in only one respect. The GI in charge would not allow my kitbag on board with me. This had to travel by another 'gear truck', which was supposed to follow behind. These soldiers, often of Italian origin, once in charge of their own transport, occasionally took to the hills to rejoin their ancestral homes, and were seen no more. This is alas what became of the driver in charge of my kitbag. No one on that particular run ever saw his luggage again. Fortunately my inseparable friends, my book and bear, were with me, so that the loss of all my possessions did not worry me unduly at the time. The day would come when I mourned them bitterly, but like the grasshopper in La Fontaine's fable, while the sun shone, I was happy to bumble along without a care in the world.

For eight hours we bounced and leapt and sprang about on the craggy shoulders of the Apennines along Highway 65, where armies had crossed backwards and forwards in pursuit of each other with heavy artillery, and with intensive bombing from the air. Our truck went from one pothole to another, swaying wildly on its creaking springs, while in the back we were hurled about in the usual manner. It is a wonder the vehicle didn't disintegrate into a pile of nuts and bolts at the bottom of a mine crater. By the time we reached Bologna, my companions and I were black and blue all over, and aching in every bone.

A visit to the Town Major provided me with a sandwich and a bed for the night, as well as a corner in the back of a PU going to Ferrara the next day. By then the country was flat and we bowled along, easily by-passing the craters in our small vehicle. On both sides of the road, gutted tanks and burnt-out aircraft lay upside down in the fields, with the wreck of blown-up trucks strewn among them. And sprouting all round, through the twisted steel and far-flung remains of battle, bloomed thousands of poppies, jauntily nodding on their stalks, in great splashes of bright scarlet, reminiscent of other terrible battlefields of twenty years before.

The villages through which we drove were less badly damaged than in the south, where the fighting for each house, street and pile of rubble had been savage and bitter. By the time this particular stretch of open road was reached, the enemy was retreating headlong towards the north, only taking time to blow up the bridges in its wake. Every time we reached one of the innumerable streams or canals with which this part of the country is intersected, we trundled over a Bailey Bridge resting on its pontoons in the water. At Ferrara, the Town Major knew of an army convoy from Milan, which was having its tea-break outside the town, on the road to the north. It was all fitting in like a jigsaw puzzle.

The entrance to Venice was protected by a military checkpoint which wanted to know your business. After stating mine I was told to find my way down the Grand Canal as far as the Morosini Palace, which was known to have something to do with our 'queer unit'. And with this information I was handed a sheet of paper, printed with the standard rate for gondola fares. Anything in excess of these prices would be exorbitant racketeering and was not to be permitted. So, armed with my bear and *War and*

Peace for sole luggage, I jumped into a gondola bound for the Morosini Palace. The sweep of the Grand Canal, with its great mansions on either side, was more extravagantly spectacular than I had ever imagined. All those palaces with Gothic windows and landing stages flanked by gaily decorated posts like maypoles, looked more like an elaborate stage-set than real life. Dressed entirely in black, the gondolier plied his single oar and I, sitting back against the cushions in my crumpled army shirt and skirt, felt incongruous in these surroundings. Nevertheless we advanced in stately and dignified progress. But all grandeur apart, what struck me most was the blessed silence of this place. No traffic, none of the shouting and hooting of other Italian towns, just the gentle lapping of the water, as gondolas glided past in a creamy froth churned up by the oars in their wake.

At the Morosini, a valet in a striped black and yellow waistcoat, who hauled me out of my gondola, announced that the Capitano was in his office. We set off up an enormous marble staircase with statues on every step, and huge wall mosaics on either side. On the first landing, tall narrow windows flanked by slender colonnades looked out over the Grand Canal. The striped waistcoat ahead of me opened an enormous studded door and stood back for me to enter.

A huge room, with painted ceiling and frescoes on the walls, opened up before me. In the centre stood a small kitchen table, and against the wall was an army camp bed covered by a khaki blanket, with a couple of faces peering out of one end.

'Come in, come in,' said one of the faces in welcoming tones. The Captain, who was tucked up in the camp bed with his secretary, hopped out, fully dressed in shirt and shorts. 'We felt a bit chilly, so we got under the blanket to warm up,' he explained. *Chilly?* At the beginning of June! Ah well, the checkpoint *had* described us as a queer unit . . .

I told him that I was reporting for duty in the News Section.

'That's old Peel-Yates. He certainly does need help. He's on his own. You'd better go and see him right away. You'll find him at the printing works, just off San Marco.'

'Fine,' I said, 'and where shall I live? Where is the PWB Mess?'

'Nothing like that here, I'm afraid. Haven't you got any friends you can kip down with?'

'I don't know who is here. Anyway, I would *much* rather be on my own. I don't mind how uncomfortably.'

'If you really mean that, you can stay here for the time being. Bags of room. Serafino will find you a corner. And we eat at the Luna.' So I found myself parked in a sumptuous reception room on the first floor, with massive crystal chandeliers, painted ceiling and marble walls, and not a single stick of furniture in sight.

'Ecco, signorina,' said Serafino proudly.

'Bellissimo, but do I sleep on the floor?'

'I will ask the Capitano for a bed for you.' And with that he vanished, to reappear five minutes later with a camp bed, a pillow and an army blanket.

All the time I was at the Morosini, this was the only furniture I ever saw in that magnificent room. But Serafino appeared every morning with a cup of tea, and whipped my scruffy sandals away for a spit and polish. My total lack of luggage seemed in no way to surprise him. Twice a week, while I was fast asleep, my khaki shirt and skirt were spirited away to be returned washed and ironed, with the morning tea. Serafino, an old family servant left behind to keep an eye on his master's property, was a pearl beyond compare.

Portly Lieutenant Stephen Peel-Yates, my new boss, though only in his early thirties, was grey-haired and mature-looking, so tall that normal human beings, unable to see the pips on his shoulder, assumed him to be of much higher rank. There was a tale he told of an occasion when a Major he once met consistently addressed him as Colonel, so that the poor elderly-looking Subaltern was unable to sit down until that officer had disappeared from the scene.

Stephen was much relieved at my arrival. All he wanted to do was to sit in his tiny office with the blinds down to keep out flies and heat, while controlling the output of the printing press which thundered away on the ground floor, shaking the building to the depths of its muddy roots. But the machinery, in order to be kept chugging busily throughout the night, had to be fed a consistent diet of stories for the local newspapers. And trundling about the countryside in search of copy was not this ponderous officer's idea of a good life. So that was where I came in useful, and explained his warm welcome.

When he had finished explaining the situation in Venice itself and the surrounding country, with its droves of dissatisfied, trigger-happy Partisans, he added (which came as no surprise to me) that no form of transport was available, and I would have to find my way around. This meant, in my experience, having to make friends with as many people as possible. Hanging around the military checkpoint at the entrance to Venice proved to be the most profitable spot of all. Here, you could pick up lifts to all the military centres in Northern Italy. What was more tricky was to persuade some officer, or other rank, to deflect his vehicle (often an unwieldy three-tonner) into the wilds of outlying villages, where a concert or a country ball was to take place, and you knew the Partisans would stage some demonstration, heads would be shaved, perhaps a riot would take place, and you could be sure of coming away with a good juicy story for Steve's printing press.

On the strength of these continual lifts, some relationships inevitably struck a root or two, when the same vehicle turned up at fairly frequent intervals. Among my regulars was a young Artillery Captain based in Verona, who came into Venice at least once a week. Apparently with unlimited time at his disposal, he appeared quite happy to drive me wherever I needed to go, with a basket of delicious cucumber and egg sandwiches in the back of his PU. Rather a dull young man, he was nevertheless well disposed, and extremely useful, particular as the only price he extracted for these continual lifts was Sunday lunch at the Lido.

Unless you had access to a private launch, the only way to get there at that time was by gondola, a very agreeable but time-consuming mode of travel. In the centre of the lagoon was the Island of San Giorgio, upon whose northern shore was perched a lunatic asylum, in which were locked up all the loonies of the town and its surroundings. As you passed in your gondola, these unhappy creatures, men and women all mixed up together, would crowd at the barred windows, looking like some gruesome Goya painting, and screaming obscenities to the world at large. Nobody knew how long they had been there, but one thing was certain—they would never get out again.

Venice, approached by a causeway four kilometres long, is built on three hundred islands, all joined together with a great number of small bridges. Although it became one of the most prosperous and beautiful cities of the Middle Ages, it started from modest beginnings in the fifth century, when a few tribesmen were driven on to the muddy islands, by invading bands from the north. No agriculture being possible on these desolate mud flats, the new inhabitants resolutely turned towards the sea to extract its riches, and by producing salt in a country notoriously short of this commodity, they soon accumulated enough wealth to consolidate their islands and drain the intervening channels, to help shipping and cut down the risk of floods at high tide.

By the twelfth century, Venice was the most powerful

[147]

city in the Mediterranean world. San Marco, built a hundred years earlier, shows the Byzantine influence prevalent at the time, with its profusion of cupolas and the incredible richness of the mosaics on their background of gold, while the elegance and dignity of the palaces date mostly from the thirteenth and fourteenth centuries, when the powerful city dominated the entire Mediterranean world. Life at the time, with its processions, colour, music and frequent celebrations in full regalia, was a magnificent affair, as we can see from contemporary paintings by Veronese, Titian, Tintoretto and others. The city's astounding wealth was built up by sheer hard work, great artistic imagination, a genius for trade, and unmitigated dedication to the common cause.

After the 56th Division had liberated the town, the newly installed Military Government had a job to persuade the Partisans who, on departure of the Germans, had moved in and ruled with a rod of iron, blood and fear, to hand over their powers. Their contribution to final victory in Italy was undeniable, and they had so enjoyed their Robin Hood activities that an ordinary peacetime life now seemed unbearably dull, so for some time after the Allied authorities had taken over, Partisan justice continued to operate in the narrow little canals, tucked away in the further islands, and corpses were often found floating downstream with their hands tied behind their backs. Girls who had befriended German soldiers could always be told by their shaven heads, and far more savage punishment was dealt out in the more distant villages, where the poor creatures sometimes had their breasts sliced off with butchers' knives. If wars are unspeakably horrible, their aftermath is often not much prettier either.

To begin with, these Partisans often struck terror into my own heart, and it was some time before I realised that, armed with my notebook and pencil, my safest weapons, there was nothing to fear. They loved publicity and were enthusiastically co-operative as soon as they heard that their exploits would be making tomorrow's news. There were endless tales of bold deeds, dashing achievement in the face of grave peril, continual sabotage of enemy equipment at the risk of their own lives—in short, they made it plain that the Allies could never have won the war without them. Living like outlaws in the mountains, and often working with our own cloak-and-dagger boys behind enemy lines, they had set up well-organised underground routes for escaped prisoners to rejoin their own lines.

After a time I even came to enjoy walking down the streets of war-ruined villages, surrounded by a troupe of these fearsome-looking brigands in their Tyrolean hats, red neck-scarves, a dozen hand grenades dangling from the waist, a couple of unsheathed knives clanking against the thigh and a sub-machine gun tucked up under one arm. But when they insisted on showing me their pride and joy, in the shape of starved, hollow-eyed prisoners tied together with rope and staked to the ground in the full blast of the sun, I could hardly keep back my tears at the terrible cruelty of it all. Often, I knew quite well, some of these men's worst crimes had been rivalry over a girl-friend, or the object of some private feud, and nothing whatever to do with war crimes of any kind.

Sometimes owing to lack of transport, these trips lasted two or three days, and I had to stay in the local taverna, sharing my hosts' ewe cheese and black bread, as well as their fleas, their geese and their hens, for we all dossed down together in the only room at the inn. Finally, if no military vehicle happened to pass through, someone would give me a lift in a mule cart to the next crossroads. And in the end I got back to Steve's office, bitten to the marrow-bone jelly by the fiercest bugs and the most ravening mosquitoes I had ever come across, and badly needing a bath, but with a notebook bursting with eye-witness stories for his ever-hungry printing press.

After a few weeks of 'country work', my boss despatched me to the local prisons, to check up on what was going on there. And *that* was a shock not easily forgotten. Tucked away behind the Doge's Palace and connected to it by the Bridge of Sighs, the medieval cells were actually *below* water level, so that the prisoners dabbled up to their knees in foul-smelling, stagnant sewage. And there they had been since their arrest by the Partisans, after the departure of the Germans, not convicted of anything specific except the usual convenient collaboration charge, and awaiting trial. My report after this first visit was so vehement that Steve tackled me about it.

'Look here, old girl, that story of yours about the prisons...'

'Yes, what about it?' I asked, bristling belligerently.

'Well, it can't possibly go through as it is, you know. You'll have to tone it down. All that stuff about swollen spongy knees, and the men paddling about in sewer water, fighting off the rats ...'

'It's the truth. You don't expect me to write lies, do you?'

'All right, all right, keep your hair on. I'm not doubting your word. It's just got to be watered down a bit. You know the Partisans. We can't have trouble with them now.'

Infiltrated as they were by a great number of communists, we knew that the Partisans were permanently on the look-out for slights and criticism. They were at the heart of a political problem, the intricacies of which were beyond my comprehension.

'Anyway,' Steve concluded, 'this question of the prisoners must be dealt with by Italian justice.'

'Italian *justice!*' I said bitterly. Two or three times a week, early in the morning, Serafino called me a gondola into which I climbed en route for the Law Courts, on the other side of the Grand Canal. The first time I attended one of these trials, I could hardly refrain from standing up and shouting at the Judge.

As I arrived, people were streaming in and packing into the court room, squatting all over the floor and standing three-deep on the benches. The prisoner was then wheeled into the room, crouching on a stool inside a cage only just large enough to contain him. Old shoes and imprecations were hurled at him as he passed, and a couple of empty bottles, bursting like bombs, exploded against the bars of the cage.

Counsel for the Prosecution (there appeared to be no Defence), a portly and self-important personage in a Doge's hat, stood up and began to harangue the court on the subject of his own virtue and rectitude throughout the German occupation. His peroration, which the Judge allowed to continue for an hour, had nothing whatever to do with the case. It was during the second hour that he charged the man in the cage with every crime in Christendom. There was no specific accusation, no witnesses, and as I say, no Defence. This man was plainly a scapegoat, brought in to be loaded with the common guilt from which almost every Italian suffered to a certain extent.

In the cage, the prisoner, slumped forward on his stool with his head in his hands, was the picture of hopelessness and despair. He knew as well as we all did that he hadn't got a chance. The trial was a travesty, the outcome a foregone conclusion. Boiling with outraged indignation, I hissed into the ear of an Italian journalist beside me, 'They are not giving him a chance. This is not a fair trial.'

'He's a bad man, signorina, don't worry about him. He deserves to die.'

'But he can't even defend himself!'

'There is no forgiveness for his crimes.'

'Why is he in a cage?'

'That's for his own protection. The people would tear him to pieces otherwise.' Remembering how, in Milan,

[151]

they had strung the corpses of Mussolini and his mistress upside down in public, I could well believe it.

'What will happen to him?' I asked, although I already knew the answer.

'He will be condemned to death,' said the journalist smugly.

And of course he was, to the insane cheers of the audience in the court, who then bustled off triumphantly to a fat lunch of pasta and vino rosso. My report of that trial, as of many which followed, took a good deal of 'toning' down before Steve would let it go through his presses.

At other times I climbed into a PU with Major Coates-Preedy, the Allied Military Magistrate for the Province, and we set off into the scorched countryside to attend the dusty, fly-blown empty local courts. These, dealing with petty theft, black market offences, and other village incidents involving no collaboration with the Germans at any time, were comical rather than tragic occasions, not even attracting the interest of those who had nothing better to do all day long than come and stare. Most people were up to similar tricks, and these were just the unlucky ones who had been caught red-handed.

But lovely Venice was not all hard work and harrowing experiences. After turning in my copy to my boss in the evening, my favourite pastime was sitting on the terrace of Florian's Café, and watching the thousands of pigeons wheeling round above San Marco Square, always in the same direction, and the crowds wandering about what has been described as the drawing-room of Europe. This could properly be extended to the world, now that servicemen of all the continents mixed with the local inhabitants. There were South Africans and New Zealanders, Americans and Brazilians, Poles, Frenchmen, Indians and Rhodesians, to say nothing of course of our own men.

Then came the great day when the cathedral was uncovered, and the boards which had protected the face of

San Marco were ceremoniously ripped away, and the famous horses and the lions were restored to their columns, their ledges and their plinths. The whole town was gathered in the square for the occasion, a military band played all the National Anthems, and the RAF staged an impressive fly-past. After that it felt well and truly like the end of the war, and the beginning of a new life of peace and hope.

Compared with Rome, much as I loved her, Venice was an extraordinarily restrained and orderly city, once the Partisans had withdrawn to their mountain fastnesses. There was very little crime, and although I was often out late at night, coming home along the narrow back canals, from a party or an opera at the Fenice Theatre, I never once had to use my hatpin. In this way, as in so many others, Venice was unique. There was a wonderfully friendly, almost a family atmosphere, with people out in their gondolas, or strolling along the quay outside the Daniele, singing and laughing and shouting all through the night, and even though the heat by August was intense, a little breeze always rustled around the lagoon, which acted as a vast air-conditioning reservoir in the centre of the town.

Field Security had, for reasons of their own, interned the owner of Harry's Bar, and all the various organisations stationed in Venice used his yacht in turn. As PWB seemed to get a good share of it, we frequently sailed away beyond the Lido as far as we dared, never too sure where the mine-fields started. These were heavenly burning hot days, jumping in and out of the Adriatic while the boat stood at anchor in deep water. When the Bora was tearing down its narrow draught funnel from the icy passes and glaciers of the Austrian Alps, we sailed hard into the wind, all leaning out of one side of the boat.

The Field Security sergeants, who had done such a good deal over Harry's boat, all boys of nineteen or twenty, were tremendous fun to be with, and I spent a great deal of my free time in their Mess, which was forever ringing with ribald laughter at somebody's shocking story of a lewd or outrageous experience. As clever as monkeys, they all spoke several languages, as well as local dialects without the slightest trace of accent, and dotty conversations were carried on from one table to another in Serbo-Croat, or the Venice patois, little bits of Basque or Provençal, or Pidgin Moroccan, all of which caused a great deal of mirth. Their Commanding Officer, who was not much older than we were, sometimes stood watching us from the doorway, looking rather wistful, perhaps wishing that he could join us. But of course as an officer, this was out of the question. I, being only an 'assimilated' one, and therefore not subject to military discipline, could slot in anywhere I fancied.

Once, when it was their turn to have Harry's impounded yacht, we all sailed off to Murano, the glass-making island, where we spent the afternoon watching the craftsmen spoon out blobs of 'metal', or molten glass, from a huge seething cauldron filled with the glowing red liquid. With a huge pair of tongs, the man tweaked the red hardening lump here and there, and within seconds a prancing horse stood on a wooden table, which burst into flames on contact with his fiery hooves. Vases, bottles, lampshades and glasses were blown out from the end of a long tube, and a huge crystal ball, as thin as tissue paper, was spun specially for me, which splintered asunder when placed in my hands.

We sailed home loaded with fragile presents for all our friends, and after an hilarious dinner in their Mess, we climbed to the roof, where we sat under the stars in the dark, while they played their guitars and crooned obscure medieval ditties. As Venice has no gardens or terraces, almost every house is topped with a wooden structure forming a platform, upon which the Venetians relax in the cool of the evening, with squeeze-box, mouth organ and guitar. Sitting there among the rooftops, and with all those musical instruments tinkling and humming and twanging away, you could dream yourself back into the days of Marco Polo with no effort at all.

The Captain from Verona who was so accommodating about lifts, one day turned up with a present of a minute mongrel puppy whose name, he said, was Brownie. Not caring too much for this name, and without realising I had a female on my hands, I changed it to Browning. When my mistake was pointed out, I saw no reason for another change, so Browning she remained for the rest of our lives together. Perky and full of self-confidence, her ears stuck out forward, flopping over her eyebrows, and with her hind legs buried to the knee in feathery, downy fur which looked like a ballet dancer's skirt, she never doubted that everybody would fall in love with her at first sight.

This, alas, wasn't always the case, and she certainly added considerable complications to my life at times. Sailing in Harry's boat made her dreadfully sick, and she took an instant dislike to Mess officers. Never bothering to hide her feelings, she would catch hold of their trousers and strenuously try to rip them off. In the end I found it politic to carry her about indoors, but as she was no lapdog, we had severe differences of opinion on the subject. On our rounds she stuck to me closely, trotting a few feet ahead, waggling her fluffy little white skirt from side to side and turning round every few minutes to make sure that I was following in her footsteps and not straying from the path. At the Luna Hotel where we had our meals, we paid a diplomatic visit to the kitchen every day, to pay our respects to the chef, and were usually rewarded by a dishful of dainty scraps, or sometimes a thighbone of such enormous proportions that we raised quite a little buzz of interest walking back through the lounge dragging it along the carpet between our teeth.

Among Browning's many accomplishments was a natural talent for swimming which undoubtedly saved her life one evening when we set off across the lagoon in the Press launch.

There was a party on the Island of the Giudecca. After sweeping across the water in a giddy loop and raising a hideous backwash which infuriated the gondoliers, we were approaching the landing stage when suddenly a blinding flash burst out of the engine. There was a simultaneous bang, and off we all flew in various directions with fragments of the launch. Browning's vociferous yaps of protest reassured me about her safety at once. After a few minutes of floundering and spluttering about through the wreckage and a heavy layer of black stinking oil on the water, we counted our numbers, and realised how lucky we had been. No casualties, not even walking wounded. Paddling ashore, we dragged one another out, and covered with engine oil, soaked to the marrow, bedraggled, stunned and shaky, we presented ourselves to our host, with a rat-like Browning prancing in the lead. Hamish Erskine was in the hall of his villa as his gruesome guests trooped in.

'Children . . .' he exclaimed. 'Oh, never mind. Come on, quick. The girls this way. The men over there.' And we were bundled into a couple of bathrooms where we were able to scrub down and discard our oily clothes. I spent the rest of the evening in an elegant Egyptian caftan, far more becoming than my eternal khaki-drill shirt and skirt.

The parties at the Giudecca were always civilised, with a properly laid table and correct *placement*, and the kind of cuisine which certainly didn't originate with the Army Quartermaster. Anyone who drank himself into a bore was blacklisted and never asked again. Sometimes, when we had talked late into the night, Hamish would say, 'Why don't you stay? You've got all you need, your book and your face, haven't you?' To which I always said yes, although I didn't bother much in those days with a face. It had to get by with sunburn and tapwater, which made life much easier under the conditions in which we lived. In the morning the batman would bring in tea and draw your curtains and run your bath. In the dining-room which smelt of toast and fried bacon, breakfast was kept hot on the sideboard, and you could have been in a well-run country house in England.

Hamish was a man of infinite resourcefulness. The story of his escape from prisoner-of-war camp in Italy, which he told me in serial form through several evenings, would fill a book. One of my favourite instalments was about the time when he was just about to rejoin our lines. There was still a bridge to cross before he was home, and up and down that bridge stamped a German soldier with a rifle and fixed bayonet. Weak as he was from his long confine-ment, his march through enemy-infested country and lack of food, Hamish knew that he didn't stand a chance in hand-to-hand combat. As the soldier drew near, he allowed himself to be glimpsed, then promptly dropped his trousers and squatted in the grass. His suspicions aroused, the German approached and peered down at this curious apparition. Covered with confusion and blushing to the roots he muttered 'Verzeihung', turned on his heel and retreated. At this point Hamish, leaping like a panther, hurtled into the man's legs, and brought him down. What followed was war work, ordinary everyday soldier's busi-ness. And that is how Captain Hamish Erskine of the Cold-stream Guard crossed the last bridge to freedom and rejoined his regiment.

When he left the Giudecca, and our new Commanding Officer established his quarters there, life changed over-night so you wouldn't know it was the same place, and you had to pinch yourself to remember the good old days. A big man with a generous, expansive, extrovert, Irish heart, the Colonel liked to think of us all as his children, and expected our evenings to be spent under his wing at the Villa. Going out with someone else, or to another party, was regarded as faintly disloyal, and definitely frowned upon.

In other words, he needed a court around him all the time. Full of his role as paterfamilias, he invited me to move into his villa altogether and give up my room at the Daniele where I had recently been billeted. Appalled by this suggestion, I turned it down ungratefully, in dire dread of losing all my precious freedom and independence. Marooned on the island without a boat of my own, I would be entirely at the mercy of the Colonel and his launch. The thought turned me cold. Going to his parties was quite another matter, and I always went whenever I was sure of a lift home. His guests, usually wild and un-predictable, were great fun, and you never knew what was going to happen next. But one thing was certain. You were never bored.

After dinner one night (no more laid table, you just helped yourself to whatever you could find in the kitchen), when a great deal of Chianti had been swallowed, the CO suddenly announced that we were going for a swim. He was immensely proud of his private beach at the end of the garden. As I protested feebly that I hadn't brought my bathing things, he said, 'You don't need anything. Every-body swims in the nude here. Stick to me and you'll be quite safe.' So off we trotted through the garden, some more steady than others, under the large flat summer moon. A few stone steps led down to the lovely white sandy beach of the island.

Standing by the water, I watched them peel off their clothes and scatter them around in all directions. The CO, stark naked and covered with a thick black doormat from neck to crotch, seized me by the elbow, 'Come along,' he said, 'get these things off, and we will lead them in.' And he started to unbutton my shirt. Tearing away from him, I pelted down the beach, shouting, 'I'm not undressing in front of you, not on your life!'

At what I considered a suitable distance I stopped, wriggled out of my clothes and ran into the sea. It was warm and bubbling with luminous froth. Diving under, I swam along the bottom as long as I could, then floated upwards on my back. The water, all misty with diffused moonlight, looked like liquid Lalique glass. It was delicious to roll about in, with the clip-clop of the tiny waves lapping all round.

After a while, as the others began to stagger out of the water in the distance, I turned towards the shore. To my amazement, a figure was sitting perched upon my clothes. *Who* could it be? Not one of our party, to be sure. Nobody would have bothered to follow me in my seclusion. This was not just annoying, it was damn cheek as well. Creeping slowly out of the water, I flopped on my belly to examine the situation. The figure outlined in the moonlight was undoubtedly that of a man. We faced each other and he stared back at me in silence. After a while he calmly lit a cigarette, blowing the smoke insolently up in the air. This was *too* much. Boiling with indignation I boldly stalked out of the water and marched up to him. Suddenly realising it was a British soldier, I saw the three stripes on his sleeve. We'll see about that, I snarled to myself, and in my most suave tones, I said aloud, 'Excuse me, Sergeant, would you mind getting off my clothes?'

The sound of my voice acted like a starter gun. Leaping to his feet with a gasp, he bolted down the beach like a hunted stag. No doubt expecting a signorina to arise from the waves, and in the hopes of a bit of a frolic, the sound of an English voice must have given him quite a turn. Once more safe in my clothes, I ran down the beach to join the others, who were now all out of the water. Staggering and falling about, convulsed and rocking with laughter at their

[159]

irresistibly comical antics, they were hurling bits of clothing at one another, then collapsing in the sand, quite overcome by the hilarious situation. A 9th Lancer was mincing around in a pair of cami-knickers (that quaint extinct wartime garment), while a Grenadier pranced about stark naked with a bra threaded over his left arm.

I don't suppose that any of them ever saw their own clothes again, but thinking of the batmen (on the old principle of *pas devant les domestiques*), I tried at least to sort them out into attire suited to their own sex. The batmen, dear souls, had I but known it, had seen far worse, and were quite able to take their cami-knickered officers in their stride. The Colonel, disdaining to dress and dangling his shorts between two fingers, loped along the sand like some huge furry satyr, leading his troupe back to the Villa.

Nobody that night got home at all, and without a lift, I had to doss down where I could. A bottle of gin was produced, and soon the party was in full swing again.

One of the first things I always did on entering a new place, whether Mess, or party, or newsroom, was a quick survey of the premises for possible sleeping corners in case of emergency. In those days I could drop off anywhere at a moment's notice, from the top of a pile of mail bags in a transport plane, to a dusty floor in an army depot, or the back of a three-tonner bumping along the potholes of a recently bombed mountain road. And once, on a long hitch-hike from Naples to Rome, I had a perfectly good snooze perched on top of a pile of sacks which I assumed to be filled with army boots, but turned out to be a consignment of hand grenades on their way to the front line. With a toothbrush, *War and Peace*, and this blessed talent, any spot on earth could turn into home at the drop of a hat, or rather, an eyelid.

As I was now quite ready to turn in, I climbed onto a narrow horsehair sofa in the furthest corner of the hall, and settled as best I could with a cushion over my head to keep out some of the noise. The last thing I saw before dropping off was a nude girl dancing by herself in the middle of the floor with her long, dark, wet hair flapping around her shoulders. There was a glorious pagan look about it all.

The rising sun, climbing over the edge of the Doge's Palace, hit me straight in the eye as I sat up at the sound of bells crashing through my head from Santa Maria della Salute next door. Empty bottles, bits of clothing, glasses lay around everywhere, but of my fellow guests, there was no sign. The servants not being up yet, the door was still locked, so I climbed out of the window and went down to the boatmen's steps on the jetty. And there I sat in the warmth of the new day, watching the sun light up the dome of San Marco with flickering flashes of gold. The lapping water of the lagoon caught little sparks of it as well. I would have been quite happy to sit there all day, watching the seabirds looping about, and the vegetable gondolas floating down the Grand Canal, shouting their wares, and the housewives letting down baskets on strings, to be loaded up with tomatoes and green peppers, and live chickens and huge water melons. But eventually a gondolier spotted me from the other side, and came paddling over to collect me. The time had come to get back to the Daniele for a bath and breakfast, and then, alas, a spot of work.

An American Captain who had recently joined our unit in one of the (to me) mysterious technical sections of PWB, approached me one day in the bar of the Luna as I was lapping a glass of my favourite cocktail, a mixture of condensed milk and some liqueur or other, which we called an Alexander. Although we hardly knew each other he said out of the blue, 'What you say we go to Milan for the weekend?'

'Hurray, what a good idea!' was my immediate re-action. I had never been to Milan, and this might be my only chance. Also I knew that Joy was there, and it would be fun to see her again. And then a thought struck me. 'What's the snag?' I asked suspiciously.

'I want someone to drive me there. Some of the guys are giving a party tonight, and I won't feel up to all that driving tomorrow.' Americans always used to set out to a party *in order* to get drunk, and the sooner they sank into that state, the happier they were.

'But I can't drive,' I said disappointed.

'Don't worry. You'll know how by the time we get there.'

So bright and early the next morning we jumped into a gondola which bore us along to the military checkpoint where his car, a captured German vehicle, was parked. An Opel Kapitän in perfect condition (which was just as well considering the terrible beating it was about to take), it was made for mountain roads, and my Captain assured me through the thickness of his hangover that it was as safe as hell. He then proceeded to confuse me hopelessly over the gears, the clutch and the brakes, then promptly fell asleep. After a series of false starts involving various com-binations of the controls, I managed with a great surge of triumph, to get the engine going, and we were off. After a few more experiments, not all successful, I finally got into third gear, and decided to stick there.

Apart from an Army convoy a mile long, with its despatch riders buzzing back and forth along the column like angry bumble bees, there was mercifully no traffic on the road. We chugged unharmed through Vicenza, Verona, Padua, and an awful lot of empty countryside in the wide-open spaces of the Po Valley. It was several hours since we had set off, and I was beginning to feel a bit restive. For one thing, as I desperately wanted to spend a penny, my predicament was acute. Embarrassment, dread of waking him up, not wanting to look a fool (I had completely forgotten how to stop the car), all combined to make me put it off as long as possible.

Finally I decided to wake him up. 'What's the matter?' he asked crossly.

'I can't remember how to stop the car.'

'What the hell do you want to stop for?'

'Well, if you must know, I want to go to the bathroom.' (Wanting a pee would have shocked him to the depths of his sensitive soul.)

'Oh for Chrissake! Well, just put your foot on the brake. You'll soon find out.' The engine stalled, and we jolted to an abrupt stop.

When we finally arrived in Milan, we discovered the PWB Mess next door to the cathedral. From the roof you had a perfect view of all the amazing gothickeries and curlicues, the myriad props and flying buttresses of the extraordinary building. Birds swooped in and out of the lacework, a perfect practice ground for training their young in the intricacies of aerobatics.

When I went in to lunch there was Joy, cool and twinkling, at a table by herself. 'Oh, Joy,' I exclaimed, sitting down next to her. 'How lovely to see you.' For the next hour we prattled non-stop, exchanging news and bits of gossip, who was where and doing what, and who was currently living with whom. It was just like an ordinary girls' lunch in a London restaurant, except that here the tablecloth was stained with wine, OK sauce and tomato soup, the waiters were rough and offhand, and the usual squalor of PWB messes prevailed all round. As the tea-coloured coffee was slurped in front of us, my American Captain came over to our table. I introduced him to Joy, and asked him to sit down. But he wasn't interested in our company. 'I want to go to Como tomorrow. Will you drive me there?'

'Of course,' I said, delighted, 'if you know the way.'

'I didn't know you could drive,' Joy remarked with surprise.

'I learnt today on the way from Venice,' I answered proudly.

The next morning *two* slit-eyed, spongy-faced captains lumbered into the hall where I was waiting, spot on time, for my fare.

'This is my friend, Buckmaster Sepp,' said my bleary-eyed Captain. 'He is coming along with us.'

'How do you do,' I said, regarding him with some alarm. Huge, fat and squashy, he seemed loose and disconnected. My Captain, who appeared to love him dearly, packed him into the back of the car. They both fell asleep instantly. In a way this was a relief as it allowed me more freedom of action for the various trials and experiments I would need to get the car going. After a few minutes only this time, we were off.

Como was a revelation. The Swiss mountains opposite, coming right down to the edge of the lake, hovered in a grey-blue mist, and the lake rippled in long thin wrinkles like cream on the top of milk when it is being skimmed. I was longing to get a boat and paddle myself on it. But my captains had other views. They made straight for the Albergo by the shore, and ordered themselves cokes and rum. An hour later they were topped up.

'Get us a boat, honey,' hiccupped Buckmaster. 'We wanna go for a row on the ocean.' Armed with a bottle apiece, they somehow managed to crawl into the boat while I took the oars and the boat boy gave us a shove with his hook. Why, oh why, I asked myself, did I always get landed with drunks? Well, said the Voice of Common-sense, which so often raised its boring head in moments of stress, you have to pay for everything, and this is the price for seeing Como.

At this point Buckmaster fell heavily on his knees and the boat gave a sideways lurch. 'C'mon, honeybunch, come and cuddle up to your lil' ol' Fatso,' he burbled as he began to crawl towards me. I gave him a great shove in the chest with the oar. 'Get the hell out of here,' I yelled, hoping to get through to him in his own jargon. 'Get back. You're upsetting the boat.' His friend made vague dabs at him to try and hoist him back on his perch. But the idea had taken root, and he had another go, this time falling heavily against the side of the boat which plunged, righted itself, then began to dance merrily about on the water. In a few minutes we were swinging round in circles. Standing up in an effort to restore the balance, I screamed at the boat boy, who was watching our antics with avid interest, on the shore, 'Aiuta, venite subito!' Leaping into another boat, he was beside us with a few deft flips of his oars.

'Back to the shore,' I panted. 'Subito, prestissimo, prego'—rattling off my emergency repertoire. And he hooked us back to safety.

'And now,' I announced with unalterable conviction, 'I am driving back to Milan. You can either stay behind or come with me as you wish.'

My Captain unfortunately had enough sense left to decide to accompany me. This time he had more trouble heaving his friend into the back. Loose limbs kept flopping out every time he tried to shut the door.

We were hardly out of the town when the back door swung open, with Buck trying to get out of the car. 'Pull him back,' I shrieked in a panic, having once more forgotten how to stop the wretched engine. My neighbour leant over and made feeble attempts at hauling him in.

'I wanna throw up,' wailed Buckmaster.

'Stop the car,' bawled the Captain. I stamped my foot on the brake, and Buck rolled into the ditch. The temptation to drive off and leave him lying there was overwhelming, but somehow I managed to keep it down. The Voice spoke up, 'Let him have his fling. He'll go to sleep after that.' Which was just what he did. But that night as I laid my weary head on the pillow, I couldn't help wondering if it had altogether been worth the price. 'Only experience will teach you what is,' said the Voice as I dropped off to sleep.

9

THE DAY FINALLY came when our job in Venice was
finished. As my friend in Algiers had said, soldiers don't
grow roots, and there was no choice but to move on.

British Armoured units, the New Zealand Division and
an Indian Brigade had occupied Trieste, after Marshal
Tito's forces had already arrived and settled in. To persuade any victorious army to withdraw from what it
regards as its lawfully acquired territory is never an easy
job, but to dislodge the Jugoslavs was, to put it mildly,
a ticklish problem. The idea was to shift them behind an
agreed frontier East of Trieste, known as the Morgan Line.
Individual soldiers, who never really accepted this new
border, were constantly trickling back, picking fights and
making a thorough nuisance of themselves.

Our news information centre in Goritsia, where Croats
and Slovenes scrapped incessantly, had been burnt to the
ground in a riot, and the trucks taking propaganda
material down to Pola, where Italians and Croats were at
each other's throats, were continually shot at. In Trieste
they spoke neither Italian nor Croat nor Slovene, but a
curious dialect called Triestini, and they meant to keep it
that way. Sick of being bossed by their neighbours, the

town now insisted on maintaining its independence and coming under the domination of no one. Whenever a little quiet reigned for a day or two, the Jugs, as we called them, worried in case things should settle down, started to stir things up in the mountains behind the town, where you couldn't possibly hope to find them and winkle them out.

The Officers' Mess in the main square of our new station, which had been occupied by Jug troops, was in an unbelievable state of filth. The lift and the baths had been used as loos, and the waiters told us that the soldiers had washed and shaved in the lavatory pans. Considering this and that, I took it rather hard when the Mess Officer told me (even *before* Browning had had a chance to get at his trousers) that he couldn't abide dogs, and if I refused to get rid of mine, I would have to go and live with the Jugoslav Delegation in the Annexe.

So off we trotted, feeling aggrieved, to the mangy little hotel round the corner, where a sullen bunch of ashen-faced delegates slunk around in a pack, never uttering a word in my presence, not for a moment doubting that I was a spy cunningly planted in their midst by the crafty Allied Military Authorities. Browning, who took an instant dislike to them, didn't help matters, particularly as she greeted the cockroach population of the hotel with evident delight. At breakfast they advanced in a body from the kitchen, then fanned out across the floor, each section taking over its own quarters at the various tables. At night they squeezed under the bedroom door and played lively games on the floor with Browning.

The Editor in charge of the News Desk of Allied Information Services, as PWB was now called, was a battered Fleet Street man with a heavily lived-in face. Kindly and easy-going, he left it to me to decide on the stories he needed. This suited me very well. The special situation in Trieste after the war made it a tricky spot, so there was always plenty going on at various levels, a good deal of hot-headed shooting, furious rows and wilful misunder-standing, and it seemed to me that every man in the prov-ince of Venezia Giulia was a law unto himself.

So, on behalf of the Allied News Service, Browning and I were once more constantly on the roads, picking up lifts wherever we could, and trudging for miles in the dust when nothing else turned up. And when I thought of the ladies of the First World War doing their bit for the soldiers and travelling around the battlefields in their chauffeur-driven Rolls, I felt distinctly under-privileged. Transport was always my most pressing problem. There were certainly plenty of jeeps and PUs swanning around on jobs not much more high-powered than mine, and per-haps by pulling strings I could have managed to get one. But knowing Admin as I did, there was time for three more wars to take place before my request would get through to the proper authority. It simply wasn't worth the trouble.

The people of the Province were violent and harsh, and considerably more ferocious than the easy-going peasants around Venice. The stony, rocky landscape itself was denuded and seared and scorched, and in the gullies of dried-up streams I sometimes came across horned vipers taking their ease in the sun, and dusty-looking tortoises lumbering about laboriously among the hot stones, hope-fully searching for water. It was an unfriendly country by nature, and the attentions of human beings had not improved it.

On one occasion, as I was returning from the Austrian frontier with an Army Captain who had given me a lift, and we had stopped by the roadside to eat our sandwiches, we decided to cross a field to find a little shade on the other side. As we approached the spot, and Browning was gam-bolling gaily ahead, the Captain suddenly froze in his tracks. 'Pick up that dog,' he ordered, 'and stay where you are. DON'T MOVE.'

'Why? What on earth is the matter?' I asked, staring at him.

He looked stiff and unnatural, and said again with great urgency, 'For God's sake call that dog back. We're in a minefield.'

'A minefield? How on earth do you know?'

'Can't you see the notice over there, MINEN?'

'For goodness' sake, why don't they mark it up properly?' I asked indignantly.

'The peasants pull up the signs for firewood. *They* know where the mines are. And they don't bother about other people.'

I called Browning and picked her up. Turning back we slowly started to walk towards the road, earnestly hoping to step into our former footfalls. The distance, which was probably only about thirty yards or so, felt like untold acres of crouching, hidden, biding menace. It was a relief to get back to the track. 'Remind me to report it to the Engineers when we get back,' was all the Captain said. 'Somebody could get blown up.'

Another time I went into Austria, where Displaced Persons, known as DPs, who had been carted around Europe by the Germans as slave labour from Poland, the Baltic States, the Balkans and various other occupied countries, were rounded up by the Allies into enormous camps, not perhaps the height of luxury, but at least providing food and shelter.

Among these unfortunate people were also thousands of Russian prisoners of war captured during the campaign, and forced to fight in the German Army against their own country. These, Russia demanded back, and whether they liked it or not, they were packed into lorries and driven to their fate in the Russian zone. Some of them, in despair at the prospect of what was in store for them, shot themselves or swallowed poison before their departure. Their plight was appalling. I couldn't understand the heartlessness of Allied policy. We had fought the war to put down oppression and tyranny, and to establish the principle of individual freedom, and now that the guns were hardly cold in the fields of battle, not only did we condone coercion, but actually fostered it as well by compelling people by force of arms to return to countries they never wished to see again. Overwhelmed by the unbelievable hypocrisy of it all, I spluttered and choked with indignation.

'What sort of freedom have we been fighting for?' I asked bitterly. The British officer who was conducting me round the camp looked unhappy.

'There's nothing we can do about it. Stalin demands these people back, and our orders from UK and America say that he mustn't be crossed in any way. We have no choice but to comply.' In other words the age-old excuse of avoiding personal responsibility, which was to become the great burning issue at the Nuremburg Trials. Were the perpetrators of atrocities, who blamed authority for their actions, guilty or not of their crimes? And the Judges found sufficient wisdom in their hearts to proclaim human beings mature enough to be held accountable for their own actions. Which is perhaps as much progress as we can hope for at the moment. As long as the signposts are there, we can at least struggle to reach them, even if we haven't yet the strength to make it. For there is no doubt that Might is still always Right, and only the fear of Stalin, the great new bully of Europe, with his persuasive million men under arms, could have forced this policy upon the West.

As I was leaving the camp at the end of the morning with a Polish officer who had invited me to lunch, we drove past a depot of captured equipment left behind by retreating armies.

'We don't know what to do with this lot,' he said with his exotic accent. 'Let's see if we can pick out a nice pair of skis for you. You're going to need them this winter.'

And so I returned to Trieste at the height of summer with a pair of Cossack skis on my shoulder.

The 56th Division, known as the Black Cats because of their arm badge, who had landed at Salerno, captured Naples, and seen bitter fighting all the way up the length of Italy, were now comfortably entrenched in the hills behind Trieste. As I had made friends with the Colonel in charge of this particular unit, I spent a lot of my free time in their Mess.

Oliver, the Colonel, and his officers had, on their arrival in Trieste, and before anybody else had time to think of it, swiftly impounded a stable of Jugoslav racehorses left behind by the Army. You really had to *know* that they were racehorses. To me they looked remarkably like a troop of lumbering medieval chargers, but of course I kept these views to myself.

Every morning at dawn, these heavy-footed monsters had to be taken up into the hills for exercise. The first time I went with them on this cavalcade, Oliver came to collect me in his jeep before daybreak. I was already dressed when he hooted outside my bedroom window, and to Browning's delight we careered through the deserted streets, screeching round blind corners and chugging up the hill to the stables in the dark.

It was a romantic-looking nineteenth-century scene, with officers saddling their horses by the light of storm lanterns held high in the air. All round, the invisible birds sang riotously, intoxicated with the thought of yet another day of searing sunshine and fat, lazy, squashy horseflies swooning right into their beaks. The great beasts neighed and snorted and pawed the ground impatiently, and a powerful smell came out of their stalls, while all round a strange, almost tangible warmth seemed to puff out of the ground. This, I knew from experience, would dissolve at daybreak and make way for the well-known early morning freshness, and all other attendant poetic accompaniments.

The Colonel leapt onto an enormous sombre-hued animal called Tito, and I was allocated the smallest they could find, a tough, mustard-coloured little brute by the name of Baby. As Mr Churchill might have said, *some* baby! From the moment I was in the saddle his one idea was to get me out of it. To begin with he set off on three legs, presumably tucking up the fourth under his belly to plague me. This awkward gait, more like that of a racing camel's than any horse I had ever met, rocked me from side to side in excruciating discomfort.

Tito was in the lead, followed by Baby and me, and Browning trotting beside us in the dark, while the other officers followed behind in single file. We were climbing a rocky mountain path, which we followed for about an hour in silence. By now the sky was milky white, and the birds switched to the second stage of their concert, less incoherent and more restrained than the former, and normally known as *the* dawn concert by those who know no better. We were in a wild and rugged part of the mountains, with great rocky boulders on one side and a copse of stunted pine trees on the other. As we reached the top of the hill, the sun came up behind the next ridge hitting us straight in the eye, and as we rode on blindly, a shot rang out in the distance, followed by a second and a third in quick succession, echoing all round the hills. The whole plateau was quivering and throbbing with sound like rolling thunder. Tito stopped, and Baby began to dance on the spot, plotting mischief.

'Keep still,' ordered Oliver. 'They're shooting at us', and turning to me he added sternly, 'Hold on to that horse. Whatever you do, don't let it rip.' All very well for him to speak, I thought to myself, with these horses bursting with oats which they can't wait to sow in the wind. But I held on with such grim determination that Baby, sensing my mood, decided to bide his time for the moment. After a few minutes we set off again, only to bring on another burst of gunfire. 'Get under the trees,' ordered the Colonel. 'We'll cross the wood and come out on the other side.'

Riding through the wild copse, tangled with low branches and thick undergrowth, was no easy matter. But when we emerged on to a high plateau with miles of stone fields stretching off in all directions, low walls dotted about for good easy jumps, and the sea, white and shimmering, miles away at the foot of the mountain, it was a glorious sight. Tito galloped away ecstatically, and Baby, throwing his rump into the air, cantered off sideways like a crab. But I was prepared, and adhered to the brute like a leech. It was not until our third ride that he managed to toss me off in the middle of a canter, head first into a pile of stones.

Sometimes we went off in the afternoon, with the sun in our backs, and nearly every time we were shot at, long before getting anywhere near the border. But these Jugs were indifferent shots, and nobody took them very seriously. Once a week the horses, thoroughly set up by their capers in the mountains, turned up on the racecourse, and gave a good account of themselves in spite of their cumbersome proportions.

Joy, who would never come on these early-morning rides because of the wind which ruffled her hair, took me instead to call on the warships in the harbour, where we drank gin in the Captain's cabin, had dinner on board, and sometimes saw a film on deck afterwards. The officers, who were gay dogs, seemed able to go ashore whenever they felt inclined. Joy and I returned their hospitality by taking them to our Officers' Club, the Little Brown Jug, a play on our nickname for the Jugoslavs, and there we danced under the stars in the garden, to the sound of the waves breaking on the rocks below. Some of our Venice friends came and went, and joined us there for dinner before disappearing again on their mysterious missions.

Occasionally we went sailing with the senior officers of the cruisers, and at other times the lieutenants borrowed the Admiral's launch, and we tore out to sea with water skis, while they did their best to knock us off our perch by veering and twisting, or suddenly stopping the boat dead in its tracks. These young officers were a boisterous lot. If ever they came across me on deck, lying in the sun reading a book, they simply picked me up by hands and feet, and hurled me into the water, book and all.

Admiral Cunningham, Commander-in-Chief of Naval Forces in the Mediterranean, dropped in on his ships for a quick visit one day. As we were all chatting in the Captain's cabin, quaffing his gin, I asked the C-in-C if I could go on a minesweeping trip for a day or two, as it would make a first-class story for our news service.

'A girl on a minesweeper!' exclaimed the C-in-C indignantly. 'Whatever next! I've never heard of such a thing.' And that, I thought, was that. But next morning, the Captain of the minesweeping fleet rang me up at my Jug annexe.

'You know that trip you wanted to go on?'

'Yes, too bad the C-in-C wouldn't have it.'

'He changed his mind after you left.'

'Oh hurray,' I yelled, leaping a foot into the air with the receiver in my hand. 'The darling man. Give him a hug for me.'

'Aye,' said the Captain, 'I'll do that. We're off on Monday morning. I'll send a rating round to pick you up at six o'clock. Don't be late or you'll miss the boat.'

The fleet consisted of fourteen ships following one another in a slanting line, and all connected together by a tough cable dragged below the surface so that, from *The Brave*, the Captain's ship, to the last man in the queue, a wide area of the sea was covered. The first and last were in the most dangerous position, exposed to the uncut mines of the field. The week before, the leading ship of another fleet had hit disaster and been blown into eternity. This time we hoped for better luck. There was a little Asdic panel with wavy lines wobbling upon it, but apart from showing it off when I arrived as the most modern piece of equipment on board, nobody paid any more attention to it from then on. Instead, perched upon various parts of the bridge, the Captain and his officers, trusting to their eyesight, were keeping vigilant watch all round. After the sailors had lowered the wire-cutting tackle into the water, some of them went to the guns, impatiently waiting for their targets to pop up.

It wasn't long before a shout of triumph went up on the bridge. 'Mine at starboard!' And at that moment we saw an enormous football covered with spikes shoot out of the water like a cork, a German K-type mine in all its glory, severed from its anchoring line by the cutting wire. After that they came up thick and fast all round. The gunners got to work, and the air was filled with thundering roars, while the mines, each one a bull's eye, exploded in all directions. On the bridge, I was dancing with excitement under the benevolent eye of the Captain. His skill in manœuvring so close to the minefield filled me with admiration. The only one who wasn't enjoying the fun was poor Browning, who simply hated the sound of the guns.

The sun was rising, searingly hot, in a perfectly clear sky and over a flat and oily sea. The time simply flew as we steamed on, with guns firing, and exploding mines shooting up huge jets of water into the air all over the sea. The Captain was able to tell through his fieldglasses whether a German or an Italian mine had popped up, and when I asked what the difference was, he gave me a demonstration by ordering the sailors to haul one of each kind right up to the boat for close inspection.

'We can have them both up on board if you like,' this most perfect of hosts offered with obliging affability.

'No thank you, that's not at all necessary,' I answered hastily.

At noon we went down to lunch in the wardroom, a merry meal with all the officers in high good humour, and no doubt to set my mind at rest, full of tales of their best friends hitting mines and going down to feed the fish. After lunch, they added, another treat was in store, for the fleet's course would skirt the Dalmatian coast, and Jug gun emplacements would take potshots at us as we snaked in and out of their jagged coastline, to show their gratitude to the Royal Navy for clearing their waters. By nightfall, and notwithstanding all these hazards, we arrived intact at our destination, where I was to spend the night, as no sleeping accommodation is provided for females on Her Majesty's minesweepers. They did things better in Nelson's Navy, when the Officer of the Watch went round the sailors' bunks early in the morning, calling out 'show a leg', and pulling out the hairy ones, while allowing the smooth ones to lie in longer.

Pola, where I was to spend the night, was a dour and shabby little fishing village at the end of a small peninsula inside Jugoslavia, with sullen, sour-faced inhabitants slinking around and silently staring at unwelcome visitors. A small and grubby hotel served as an Officers' Mess, where British soldiery came and went for an occasional night on their way in and out of the Balkans. Thither I repaired for dinner and, I hoped, a night's sound sleep.

The Captain came ashore, and we all gathered round a large circular table for our feast of fried corned beef and tinned peaches. The Balkan officers were in great form, cheap Italian wine flowed by the bottle, and the meal ended with a singing session of all the popular war tunes of the time, including, of course, *Lili Marlene*.

Soon after the Captain had gone back to his ship, I went off in search of a bed for the night. As the padrone at the reception desk assured me that no such thing was available in the hotel, or indeed in the town, I returned to the lounge next to the dining-room, pulled a couple of armchairs together, and lightly (so I thought) hopped into this roost with Browning in my arms. The chairs, which were on castors, flew apart, and we found ourselves on the floor. In the end, after various unsuccessful attempts, we ended up curled round each other *underneath* the chairs, with a tablecloth draped over the whole arrangement like a tent, to keep out, with indifferent results, mosquitoes and other intruders.

As the carousing officers gradually began to leave the dining-room, each one in turn lifted a corner of my tent to peer inside, then, rudely roaring with laughter, went out banging the door. A hostile silence reigned at last in this unwelcoming establishment, and Browning and I were left in peace to deal with all manner of infiltrating marauders, including bugs swarming out of the floor-boards, and various detachments of cockroaches nosing around for possible titbits. But, used to the rough and the smooth as we both were, we were sound asleep within a few seconds.

The next morning the Captain of *The Brave* detailed a motor torpedo boat to take me back to Trieste, and the nineteen-year-old Lieutenant who was in charge showed me how to drive it, and how many revolutions were needed for a slight veer to the left or right, I mean of course, port and starboard. We made a smooth and per-fect crossing back through yesterday's freshly swept waters, while seabirds circled round us, squawking loudly, and Browning, much relieved by the steady state of the sea and the absence of guns, joyfully cantered around the little boat, yapping at the birds overhead.

My boss was pleased with the story, which appeared with several photographs in the local press, and I was despatched forthwith to survey the German internment camp at Bolzano, where, although I didn't know it then, my aunt Mimi, the spoilt darling of our own nanny before the First World War in Australia, had been interned during *this* war. There the prisoners, many of them women, had been kept in minute cells, under the daily threat of the firing squad. And all the Alpine beauty of the little town tucked away under aromatic fir trees, surrounded by shaggy peaks sticking up like rotten teeth against the clear blue sky, was nothing but one more poignant reminder of all the pain and indignities suffered for four long years by the prisoners held there within the camp.

Since our arrival in Trieste, our 'Queer unit', being now stationed in a very inflammable zone, had been offloaded by the Foreign Office onto the broad shoulders of the War Office. We, perfectly unconcerned by the perilous state of the hot spot in which we lived, received this information with equanimity, but the War Lords were soon to wish that this particular baby hadn't been landed in their lap.

Our Commanding Officer at AIS, a handsome young Colonel with dazzling good looks, a commanding presence and a magnetic personality, whose outstanding father had been one of Mr Churchill's favourite Civil Servants, controlled the unit with firmness, unfailing good humour and a kind of inspired brilliance which kept us all under a permanent spell. Dinner in the Mess ended several evenings a week with one of his witty or soul-stirring speeches, according to the mood or the events of the moment. Among his many talents was a booming baritone which he used to great effect at the end of the speeches. The *Volga Boatmen*, when sung by him, was an experience which made you hug yourself and tingle all over. And what endeared him to me most of all was going over the head of the Mess Officer, declaring it to be quite incorrect for me to be dumped among all those dreadful Delegates in the Annexe. And Browning and I were allowed back to the Mess.

The days were growing shorter, and one more summer was coming to an end. The Bora, which had been blowing down from the Alps more and more frequently, was beginning to reach such force that ropes had to be strung along the streets for people to hang onto whenever they were picked up off their feet by the gale. I was beginning to shiver in my khaki drill uniform and open sandals. So when my boss asked one day if I would like to go to Vienna instead of him, I agreed with alacrity. He had had enough of Overseas, and was longing to get back to his own stamping ground in Fleet Street.

Oliver, who gave me a slap-up black market farewell dinner the night before I left, lent me his own very comfortable 'improved' Command Car with a seat upholstered in the back in delicate camel tones, as well as a couple of Other Rank drivers, and a picnic hamper stuffed with delicacies. And off we set at the crack of dawn for Klagenfurt. It was a long day's drive, climbing and winding in and out among the Austrian Alps, in the sharp clear air scented with pine resin. We stopped by a broad shallow stream for lunch, in which could be seen speckled trout wriggling upstream between the stones. No self-respecting British soldier was ever caught without his teapot and kettle. 'When in doubt, brew up', was the notice once seen on the back of a truck in the heat of battle during the Desert War, so now, faithful to custom, my soldiers brewed up, and we all sat back swallowing scalding mugs of tea beside our trout-filled mountain stream.

At Klagenfurt they dropped me at the Post Hotel, then departed on the long trek back to Trieste. Klagenfurt on the Wörthersee, an enormous lake surrounded by mountains, was a magic place, but I was bound for Vienna, and didn't feel justified in lingering unduly. There was just time all the same to have a quick look at the famous 'Wurm', an enormous stone dragon of great antiquity which slumbers in the main square, and is said to waggle his tail whenever a virgin walks past. And according to local legend, the tail hasn't twitched within living memory.

A truck was leaving early in the morning for Graz, the next stopping place on the long road to Vienna, and cluttered up with my unwieldy possessions, now consisting of Browning and the Cossack skis, which made some people smile and a good many others audibly swear, I climbed on board. In Austria our name was changed to Information Services Branch of the Allied Control Commission, or just ISB, ACA for short.

As the war came to an end, ex-Captain Beauclerk, who was now a Lieutenant-Colonel, working from Army Headquarters near the Austrian border, was endeavouring to set up the usual free news service to educate the liberated people of the area in democratic ways. But the Jugs who were also there, and who had seized the main printing works, had very different views on the subject. Why waste time, they wanted to know, in educating? When all you needed was good old slogans with a thumping message hitting the nail square on the head without all the useless time-consuming democratic fiddle-faddle which the Allies eccentrically went in for. 'SMRT FASCISMU' was their favourite, and what they regarded as their most convincing argument against the German menace. What indeed could be more concise than 'Death to Fascism'?

Men of few words, these Partisans were all for action. When, after their surrender, the Germans were being rounded up for disarming purposes, their numbers were so vast that no adequate escort could be found, and they were sent marching off to their various internment camps on their own. The delighted Jugs, lying in wait for them on the way, would descend with wild shrieks from their mountain hideouts, falling upon the long columns of the defeated enemy, in wild whooping gangs, and strip them bare of all possessions. To the Jugs, watches were the greatest prize, a kind of badge of honour, and that winter in Vienna I frequently saw Russian soldiers who felt the same way, proudly displaying on both arms rows of watches reaching up to the elbow.

We were strictly forbidden to enter the Russian Zone. With a special pass, not by any means granted to everybody, we were allowed to travel *through* their territory in order to reach our own region. Sometimes, for no reason at all, passes were torn up, vehicles 'confiscated' and the travellers sent back on foot through snowed-up mountains. Every day new tales of incidents in the Russian Zone came to light, and nobody undertook the journey lightly. The darlings of Roosevelt and Churchill were proving less co-operative than expected.

Graz is a charming little provincial town with a clock-tower perched on a rock in the central square, and narrow picturesque streets lined with houses painted all over with gay colourful frescoes. Our Mess there, under the control of young Major Greaves, was a haven of peace and order. Not that *he* would agree of course, but so it appeared to me after the various bear gardens in which I had lived so far.

Although I arrived with a dog well after lunch was over, nobody kicked me out on the spot, *and* a meal was miraculously produced for Browning and myself, without any grumbling or swearing. I was beginning to feel I had arrived at the wrong place, until I met the gentle, courteous Major in charge. It was obvious from then on that the influence of his personality had soaked right through to the basic foundations (kitchen and staff at least) of the Mess. In some mysterious way beyond the reach of corruption, he was one of the few human beings I had yet met whose inner strength and moral rectitude had in no way been affected by the demoralising influences and experiences of war.

IO

DURING A VISIT to the Major's office, I learnt that a convoy was assembling to confront the hazards of crossing the Russian Zone. At the end of the war, Austria had been divided into four parts, of which the Americans controlled Salzburg and Upper Austria, the French had the Tyrol and Vorarlberg, and the Russians who were allocated Lower Austria and the Burgenland, clamoured also for the territory surrounding Vienna, so that nobody could enter or leave the capital without their knowledge. For our lot we received the provinces of Styria and Carinthia in the south-east, which included a tiresome frontier with the truculent Jugoslavs.

The magic grey passes, without which no civilian ever squeezed through the Frontier Post, had been applied for in Vienna, and were expected at any moment. As these had to be brooded over by the Russian authorities at Headquarters, and receive their official stamp, it could take anything up to a week or more, and once they came, it was made abundantly clear that stops at any point on the way were strictly *verboten*.

And so we settled down to wait, and meanwhile I made friends with my convoy mates. Sir Alexander Bethune, who had been at the British Embassy in Kubitschev during the early part of the war, could speak Russian, and would act as interpreter at the frontier in case of trouble. Captain John Cox, an enigmatic and mysterious character who spoke in a soft and feathery voice, was moving up with a detachment of Austrian young ladies, who naturally became known as Cox's Orange Pippins. Among them was Gretl, who was to marry Norman Cameron in the following year. She became a life-long friend. A sprinkling of blond, handsome young men, who were somehow connected with the Pippins, made up the contingent of the convoy, which consisted of three trucks and a couple of small vehicles. All packed and ready (at least those who had something to pack), we were only waiting for the word go. This finally came through a couple of days later, when a telephone call from Vienna announced that Lieutenant Barry Evans as official Pass Bearer, would shortly be on his way, and we were to meet him at the frontier, where God (and the Russian Guards) willing, all would go swimmingly and we would sail through without further ado.

For extra safety the pretty Pippins, potentially irresistible to the wild and passionate instincts of our Slav Allies, were locked up in the back of a truck, while I, a leathery old campaigner, and in uniform anyway, was considered a lesser risk, and allowed to sit in front with Browning and the driver.

For such a haphazard arrangement, the operation was remarkably well timed. We hardly had an hour or so to wait before we saw an open jeep roaring up the road towards the barrier. Lieutenant Evans, all smothered in a huge army greatcoat, and standing up in the vehicle, was waving the passes above his head and shouting, 'Triumph, Eureka, got 'em!' Tense and apprehensive as we were, and dramatic as the situation then seemed to us, it was with exaggerated relief that we saw him materialise.

In the back of the truck the poor Pippins were holding

their breath. As the Russians had assumed the right of life
and death over the Austrian Nationals (whether legally
recognised or not, this was in fact the case), people were
continually being dragged off convoys without rhyme or
reason, and were never heard of again. The philosophy of
the Russian troops was simple and straightforward. They
didn't bother their heads with refinements of humanitarian
principles or fair play. If they wanted something, they took
it. If resistance was offered, they bashed and grabbed.
Marshal Koniev's Divisions, fighting all the way like
demons, had managed quite well without supplies, living
off the land throughout the campaign, so that his soldiers,
in good training and well practised in the art, saw no reason
for abandoning such rewarding methods at this stage.
Anyway in their eyes, the enemy who had lost the war
deserved no quarter. Knowing all this, the Pippins
trembled, and we trembled for them. But this time at least,
all was well. No objection was raised, and our convoy
rumbled through.

As soon as we had passed the frontier and were able to
relax, I began to look around and take in the surroundings.
The Semmering Pass, which was the dividing line between
the two zones, was theatrically beautiful, and whether you
liked mountains or not, you could not help being impressed
by the grandeur of the lofty peaks clad in sombre pines,
and topped with snow. The keenness of the cold, sharp
air made you long to get out and start climbing there and
then. The roads, though rough and in bad repair, were like
billiard tables compared with the war-wrecked highways
of Italy.

As fighting in Vienna had been heavy, many of the
streets were just enormous heaps of dust and rubble. It was
difficult to believe that this drab and shabby town had ever
been the glittering, dancing capital of the Congress of
Europe and of the Hapsburg Emperors. Autumn leaves
drifting off the trees, whirled about, settled on the

pavements and piles of rubble, adding an infinitely melancholy air to the already desolate aspect of the city. People in dark overcoats hurried along with hunched shoulders and blank, shut-down faces. Furtiveness, fear and suspicion were everywhere, testifying to some unknown, hidden menace.

Our convoy stopped outside the Park Hotel, where Alexander Bethune and I got out, while Captain Cox whisked his Pippins away to settle them in civilian flats. Bustling and comfortable, the Park Hotel was warm and welcoming until you reached the bedroom floors. Ice-cold and uninspiring, my room was furnished in the dismal provincial style and depressing bad taste of the Thirties. With no wish to linger, and after a hasty and abbreviated wash in cold water, I beetled downstairs to the bar to see who was there. You never knew where or when old friends would turn up.

An English girl, recently arrived from London, introduced herself, and we decided to go and explore together. As Olive had even less German or Russian than I, we thought that joining forces would be fun, and could do no harm from the security point of view. So after a quick lunch in the large, warm dining-room full of Henpeck wives and children, with their military Lords and Masters, down the Underground we went, making a note of our own station of Hietzing for future reference.

The ramshackle little train of the Stadtbahn, which rattled and clanked along on its rusty rails, was packed with surly, churlish figures bearing rucksacks upon their backs. As Vienna was a starving city, its inhabitants were continually on the move, collecting or delivering black market food and articles of barter. Once you knew your way around, you got your meat from a pram shop or the barber round the corner, fish from the dentist and sugar from the draper's, in exchange for an army blanket, or a tube of toothpaste or a second-hand pair of boots.

Gretl, No. 1 Pippin, always brimming with riveting true-life stories, told me of a friend of hers who visited the local doctor in Graz. Queueing up with a dozen other girls awaiting their turn to be parted from their little Russian or Jugoslav baby, she eventually got to the seat of action where a weeping, battered girl was crawling off the operating table.

'Get ready,' snapped the doctor. 'I haven't got all day to waste on you.' And with these words he hustled her towards the carving slab.

'But, Herr Doktor,' protested the girl.

'Come on, don't fuss, it only takes a minute,' he growled, sharpening his knives. And it was only after a desperate struggle that she managed to escape, gasping as she sped through the door, 'I was only bringing the butter and the eggs, in the bag on the table.'

Later that winter, another rucksack story, more tragic this time, caused quite a stir among the occupying forces. A Viennese doctor, who performed this service out of pity for the girls, only charging what they could afford to pay, discovered to his great distress that one of his patients had died during the operation. Losing his head, he chopped her up into bag-size pieces, which he packed into his rucksack, and at nightfall, set off on foot towards the Danube, into which he intended to tip his sinister load. As far as anyone could see, he was just another Austrian on his way to do a bit of food swopping. Having reached the bridge, he passed the Russian guard without a hitch, so with much relief he strode on, planning to unload his pack at a propitious moment. And suddenly, as in a nightmare, he heard footsteps behind him, while the soldier stamping up to him yelled Halt! in no uncertain tones. Bored on a quiet evening, and thinking to pass the time, the guard had turned back, hoping for no more than a sausage of a piece of smoked pork from that harmless-looking rucksack. What he discovered was more than he had bargained for.

Olive and I, returning from our first expedition just before dark, had seen enough to dazzle and amaze us. Walking from the Stadtpark to the Ring, and into the old medieval city, we wandered through the ancient narrow streets, with everywhere the same furtive people slinking around, and none of the nonchalant Latin love of passing the time of day out of doors. The Russian soldiers we scuttled past looked sinister in their jackboots, topped with baggy trousers and high-necked tunics, belted round the middle like mujhiks, each carrying a rifle or tommy-gun. Women soldiers, square-cut and broad-shouldered, equally accoutred apart from a skirt instead of trousers, roamed the streets as well. We saw a couple of them pick up an overturned jeep, set it on its feet and climb back into it, dusting their hands.

It was difficult to associate these people with the gentle peasants of *War and Peace*. The only scene which seemed to fit was the sight of the long flat carts pulled by a team of foaming horses, with a soldier standing at the front holding the reins in one hand, and a long whip flicking about in the other. This equipage, galloping through the cobbled streets with a deafening din, was a gloriously stirring vision.

That evening, Norman Cameron appeared in the bar of the hotel. As I had no idea that he was there, it was a very welcome surprise. After dinner, which we had together, we went into the ballroom to indulge in a spot of the special shuffle which we had perfected together in Rome. The room was crowded. Although a few familiar faces appeared here and there, there were a great many new people recently arrived from London with the Allied Commission. Norman introduced me to our Commanding Officer, in whose tracks I had unknowingly followed all the way since Norfolk House in London.

'What are you doing up here?' he asked, after inviting us to join his table.

'The AIS News Editor in Trieste asked me to come instead of him. He wanted to go home.'

'This is most tiresome. I particularly wanted *him*. There was no need for you to come up here at all,' rasped my husband-to-be in most unwelcoming tones.

'Oh dear, well I'd better go back to England. I'm due some leave anyway. It will fit in quite well.'

'You're not due anything at all,' snapped the Colonel. 'Nobody is *due* leave. It's a privilege, not a right. Let's go and dance, anyway.'

'When shall I go back to England, then?' I persisted, as we edged in among the couples on the floor.

'I didn't say you could go back,' he said sharply. 'Do concentrate now.'

The dance floor was glittering with uniforms. French officers, with revolvers bouncing on their behinds as they performed their curious hopping version of the Viennese waltzes, Russians with all the heavy ironmongery of their medals clanking and jingling upon their breasts, smooth American captains and majors gleaming like mahogany with all their polished leather and impeccable haircuts, and our own aloof, distinguished-looking officers in their trim Savile Row Service dress. And among all this elegance, I was prancing about barefoot in open sandals. Ah, mamma mia, I thought to myself. Suddenly the music changed to a Paul Jones. As the lights flickered and dimmed, and while the usual reshuffle was taking place among the dancers, it appeared that all was not well in the centre of the room, where a commotion was going on. Simultaneously a shot rang out, and a crystal chandelier exploded, raining glass splinters all round. The music stopped and we all stood still, rooted to the spot, as an apoplectic Russian officer, re-holstering his revolver, stumped angrily out of the ballroom. Unfamiliar with Paul J's, and not caring for the idea when explained to him, he simply wasn't going to have his girl whisked out of his arms during a dance.

And that was the end of my first day in Vienna.

The weather was daily growing colder, and Norman, who was well over six foot tall, realising my plight, presented me with an enormous pair of his heavy-duty battle-dress trousers, which I laboriously unstitched and sewed into a skirt. One of his vast khaki pullovers, reaching down to the knee-cap, made a warm cosy tunic, and to complete the ensemble he added a pair of his long knitted stockings, whose ends I chopped off for a snugger fit. These blunt square knitted toes, stitched together with coarse brown cotton poking out of open sandals, did tend to catch the eye on more formal occasions, but beggars can't be choosers, and I was glad to be warm, and immensely grateful to Norman for his generosity.

Since our Roman days his mood had changed. The following Sunday he rang through to my bedroom at seven o'clock in the morning. 'Good heavens,' he exclaimed, 'are you still in bed? Well, get up quick and I'll be round for you in twenty minutes. We are going to church.'

Struggling into my home-made uniform, I went down to the hall, where he was waiting for me, with his curly hair standing on end, and his enormous army greatcoat flapping around his ankles. Under the cynical eye of the hall porter, no doubt used to the impeccable turnout of German officers, we set off together into the cold November morning, bent on our Sunday devotions.

Low Mass was in progress in the first church we called at. The faithful, discouraged by the perishing cold, and few in numbers, contributed little to the atmosphere of devout sanctity which Norman was probably looking for. Altogether, it was a poor show. After a few minutes, he announced in a loud voice, 'I don't think much of this place, let's push off and find something more lively.' So, blowing on our frost-bitten fingers, we proceeded to the next church down the line. There wasn't much to be said for this one either. 'Why are all these prelates so bloody pompous?' complained Norman. 'Come on, we're wasting our time here.' And off we went once more. After three or four more visits, and still finding satisfaction nowhere, he eventually said, 'I expect you would like some breakfast?' As that was the first welcome suggestion I had heard that morning, I heartily agreed, and we dived into Sacher's blissfully warm interior, all reeking with the aroma of army sausage and toast.

Sacher's Hotel, in the Ring, had been requisitioned for senior British officers, and was at that time giving asylum to the distraught person of Nijynski, who had suddenly appeared outside Vienna, springing into the centre of a group of Russian soldiers squatting around a bonfire, one night soon after their armies had overrun Austria. And until his future could be sorted out, the British Commission, watching over him like a mother, had given him one of the best rooms in the hotel.

Over our pot of tea and substantial well-earned breakfast, Norman's disappointment over his frustrated and fruitless spiritual search evaporated, and he reverted to his usual robust and cheerful self. The following spring he fell in love with Gretl, and they were married in Vienna. But having optimistically tried to fit in too much, he found himself on the evening of his wedding day engrossed in a chess match with the Vienna Police, while his bride waited patiently far into the night for her newly wed, day-old husband.

But now, breakfast being over, he was in a reminiscent mood. 'Talking of clothes,' he remarked, eyeing the bat sleeves of my oversize khaki pullover, which hung in loose folds around my wrists, 'did I ever tell you about my swim in a German river before the war?'

Replete with sausages and tea, I leant back in my chair, ready for a good yarn.

'While I was at Oxford,' he said, 'I went on a walking tour through Bavaria during the long vac. It was terribly hot and dusty, and when I arrived at a river, and there seemed to be no one around, I took off my clothes and dived in.' The water, straight from the glaciers, was blissfully refreshing, but he had reckoned without the swiftness of the current. Halfway across, he was carried downstream like a blade of grass. Struggling desperately for the opposite bank, he was relieved to reach a bend, behind which suddenly appeared a totally unexpected village. A small jetty stuck out into the stream, and to this he hitched himself.

'There was nothing else for it,' he concluded. 'I just had to pelt down the village street with my hands over my privates, while all those stupid Krauts hustled their womenfolk into doorways bawling, "Madman! Polizei! Hilfe!"' At which point the adjoining tables in the dining-room, much to his surprise, collapsed with laughter. Looking around I could see Lord Schuster, who was in Vienna to de-Nazify the Federal Government, and disentangle Austria from the German tentacles in which she had been entwined since 1938, and Fifi Schuster, his daughter, who conducted an agreeable café existence in the Ring with her Austrian friends. A young Count Tolstoi, who was supposed to be on his way to America, sat aloof and alone at a table in the window. Lord Pakenham, on a lightning visit from England, was surrounded by an animated group of ACA officials, and further away Ross was treating his friend Honor Tracy, the writer, to coffee and Naafi cigarettes, while Benjamin Britten, firmly buttoned down behind the mask of his noncommittal face, kept his eyes on his plate, discouraging would-be chatterers. Graham Greene, also an inmate of the hotel, usually breakfasted in his room on pink champagne. At a cocktail party where he had his back to the wall, and his look of intense misery effectively kept most people away, I had approached him with the object of trying to cheer him up, but within a few minutes *I* was the one to be giggling at his stories, one of them being about John Betjeman who, at a party rather like the present one, was approached by a young lady who asked him if he liked fox-hunting. To which he replied, 'I can't even *sit* on a horse, let alone shoot from one!'

The Allied Commission was divided into several Divisions, of which the Information Branch, as part of the Political Division, was ruled over by our Commanding Officer, Colonel Charles Beauclerk. This Branch included the usual Newsdesk, a German-language newspaper called the *Weltpresse*, on which Pippin Gretl worked as a reporter, and the British *Morning News*, which was issued for the consumption of the English contingent throughout Austria. The usual radio and monitoring stations were farmed out in the Zone.

The Newsdesk, on which I found myself once more on the night shift, was now operating under the direction of Max Wilde, who had discovered in his heart a great love and admiration for the Russians. With a few words of their language at his command, he laudably did his best to chat them up on all occasions, in spite of which they appeared to regard him with as much suspicion as the rest of us. I remember a garden party at the High Commission, where Max, ever conscious of his role of peacemaker, was earnestly addressing a Russian General, who steadily fixed him with a baleful eye while consuming one vodka after another, and tossing the empty glasses over his shoulder into the bushes, where lurked a couple of agile batmen who caught them nimbly as they came flying through the air.

Although Vienna was divided into American, French, Russian and British sections, we were allowed to roam all over the town at will, as long as we didn't overstep the mark into the exclusively Russian ZONE. The constant incidents of house-breaking by the soldiers, usually followed by rape, theft and sometimes murder (there was one shocking incident where a man was done to death with a leather belt) were indignantly brought up by the Western Allies at the weekly Quadripartite meetings, without getting much change out of the Russians, who gave no reason or explanation for anything that ever happened. Everything always had to be 'Referred to Moscow', which was the last you ever heard of the matter. On one occasion, feeling myself being prodded between the shoulder-blades, I turned round to face a bayonet with which a Russian soldier was trying to shift me along. If I hadn't hopped smartly out of the way, he would undoubtedly have threaded me onto the end of his rifle. Unknowingly, I had been walking along the pavement *behind* one of their requisitioned hotels in the Ring.

That winter, a sinister feeling of menace hung over the city, stalking the streets and pervading the air, so that you didn't even feel secure in your own home. Any time of the day or night, a great battering on the door could bring doom and disaster. People, once kidnapped, were never heard of again, so that you never knew what fate to expect, and the very few who did escape, never dared tell.

Although in Rome, crime had flourished in all its multifarious aspects, here in Vienna you felt a more determined and purposeful malevolence floating in the very oxygen you breathed. Graham Greene who, on arrival in Vienna, had sniffed and soaked up the putrid atmosphere with the appreciation of a connoisseur, was frustrated for a long time at not being able to discover a theme worthy of this extraordinarily evil background, for the film script which he had come to write. Colonel Beauclerk, bringing his fertile mind to bear on the case, dredged up the Sewer Police and performed the introductions, so that Mr Greene's dilemma was solved, and the plot of *The Third Man* gradually began to take shape.

Since the Park Hotel where we lived was a long way from the ISB offices, and ACA transport was as erratic and unreliable as PWB's had been, Gretl managed to find me a flat on the floor below her own, and produced a friend who wanted to share my room, while Olive, who also moved in with us, had a tiny bedroom to herself. The remaining space consisted of a living-room, a bathroom, and the entire flat depended for sole heating on a boiler enthroned in the middle of the kitchen. As no fuel of any kind figured on the official rations, we trekked out like any other citizen, with rucksacks on our backs, to the Vienna Woods to collect sticks for our fire.

By this time I had acquired an Army officer's overcoat which, though the smallest size available, enveloped me from head to foot like a burnous. Huddled inside this garment, crouching in my seat on the Underground, bent on one of my stick-collecting excursions, I suddenly felt myself being seized by the collar and swung into the aisle, while a gruff voice growled down my ear in German, 'Out you get, young man, and make room for me.' And a bulky Viennese burgher dumped himself in my place.

Collecting sticks was a rewarding occupation, until the snow gradually began to engulf our world. As it fell more heavily and persistently over the desolate city, the hideous heaps of war rubble slowly turned into bizarre, lumpy shapes, and the outlines of jagged ruins were softened, as the whole place deceptively acquired a bogus fairytale quality. Bereft of fuel, our boiler turned stone cold, and our flat became an ice-box. Town gas came on for early birds, between four and five o'clock every morning, and we, who kept different hours, had to get used to rising at dead of night to brew a hasty pot of porridge, and race back to bed to consume it there, then drop off to sleep again until a more reasonable hour. In the evening, the gas was switched on between seven and eight, just giving us time to heat up a tin of soup or a ready-made steak and kidney pudding, which we then gobbled in the living-room with a hot-water bottle in our lap and one candle on the table.

Electric light was either kaput, or being saved up for industry.

At the weekend, Olive and I shouldered our skis, climbed into the military train to the British Zone, and spent a blissful Sunday sliding down the Kanzel in Carinthia, and chugging up to the top again in nippy little tanks, which seemed able to crawl up at almost any angle. Sometimes we trudged up to the Kahlenberg just outside Vienna where, from the top of the hill, you could see the Danube, with its banks encrusted with ice, and great ice-floes slowly snaking their way down the current, while straight ahead the snow-covered plains of Hungary stretched on for immeasurable miles, into unknown and mysterious Slavonic lands, where packs of hungry wolves galloped across the frozen wastes. At other times, we went skating in the Stadtpark, where Viennese waltzes blared out of loudspeakers looped about in the trees, and half the town gathered on the ice in their beaver hats, the whole thing looking like a lively and animated Breughel scene. In a temperature of twenty degrees below zero, your breath stuck to your balaclava helmet in little needles of ice, and the Russian soldiers who stamped past on the way to salute their newly built monument in the park, blew their noses in their fingers with a fine disregard for our more effete handkerchief habits.

After a couple of hours of energetic skating, thoughts turned with one accord to atom bombs. This was a powerful brew concocted out of gin and cherry-brandy, which warmed you up in no time, and which Johnny, the barman at Sacher's, made to perfection. After one or two of those, you felt up to anything.

Sunday lunch was a very social affair, with officers from all the Services, and civilians from the Allied Commission and the Embassy hobnobbing with visitors from Greece, the Balkans and Germany. The hangman Pierrepoint also appeared in our midst. I remember him in the bar, surrounded by a ghoulish audience avid for details of his craft.

The DP camp which I had visited the previous summer was in a continual state of agitation and despair. The concentration of human misery which prevailed in that community was high and constant. Apart from several suicides that winter, there was also a series of murders, which could not be ignored by the authorities, and as this was before the abolition of capital punishment, Pierrepoint was summoned to execute justice and teach the rudiments of his trade to hopeful budding hangmen on the spot. And when I made my usual protest about this odious practice, I was firmly told that crime must be punished by the law of the land (the DP camps being under British rule were naturally subject to its laws), and that if allowed to go unpunished, crime would become rampant, and anarchy would result.

Ross's ultra-sensitive, quivering, and often querulous aura, was tinged with a whiff of the macabre. The reason why he had never married, he told me at great length, and with a wealth of detail, was because his fiancée's head, which had been knocked off by a *horse-drawn* carriage under his very eyes, had rolled down the street and landed at his feet. From that day on, he said, whenever he looked at a woman's fair countenance, he could see those terrible eyes staring up at him from the ground.

And after the war, when he lived alone, uncared for and neglected, in a state of penury in a vast house in Cambridge, Gretl, another friend and I, decided to come to his aid. Descending on him with brooms and brushes, we spent a week scraping and scrubbing the floors, washing the curtains and painting the walls, with the object of getting some of the rooms ready for letting, to provide him with a small but steady income, in order to keep the wolf on the right side of the door. Starting from the ground floor, we rose slowly and unsteadily, until we reached a particularly cluttered bedroom. Ross, who had been keeping well away from our activities, was hovering around, all of a dither and getting in the way. Gretl, who had dived under the bed to deal with the cobwebs there, suddenly reappeared with a small box in her hands.

'Is this any use?' she asked, 'or shall I put it on the bonfire?'

Ross, rushing forward, snatched it away from her and clutched it to his bosom. 'It's my mother,' he squeaked, and rushed out of the room, straight off to the pub for comfort, with his little box in his arms.

In Vienna, he appeared in the Mess one morning with a fearsome-looking black eye. This, he explained, was due to a little accident he had suffered the night before, when his shoe had somehow jumped off his foot, and caught him a terrific wallop in the eye.

His front teeth, which were planted in eccentric fashion in his top jaw, stuck out at all sorts of unexpected angles. This had happened, apparently, on an occasion when he had fallen face forward on a railway line in a London station. After returning to England, and deciding to do something about those teeth, he had a gleaming set of gnashers fashioned to measure, and fitted to his top jaw after extraction of the originals. But apart from all the trouble taken, the fit was far from perfect. The new set, tiresomely rattling around in his mouth, kept leaping out at unexpected moments.

Once, while dining with us, they jumped out as usual, sliding under the table, where our irascible Irish Water Spaniel lay in wait, hoping for trouble. The teeth were something new. Carefully she crept forward, sniffing suspiciously, while Ross, slowed down by his alcoholic intake, also approached cautiously from the other end to retrieve his property. Holding our breath and bending low, we watched the proceedings. Inch by inch they both advanced upon the teeth, which lay grinning between them. The spaniel was baring hers, as a deep warning growl rumbled in her throat. Imperceptibly, Ross's hand hovered closer, then suddenly with an unexpected pounce, snapped over the teeth. In a second they were back in place, and we all surfaced with relief. No mention was made of the incident, and conversation resumed its interrupted flow. But those teeth were fated from the start. Ross, who enjoyed his drink, had frequent hangovers. One day, as he was quietly puking into the loo, minding his own business, the teeth, up to their usual tricks, followed suit and were seen no more. He had pulled the plug on them before realising his loss.

He was full of curious bits of knowledge, and unlikely facts dug out from goodness knows what obscure sources, and immense trouble was taken, sometimes with rather trifling results. On 1 May, in Vienna, he always gave a party in which a particular herb, which he called Waldmeister, figured largely. Steeped in a wine cup, this was meant to be a rare and esoteric experience. For days beforehand, we were despatched into the Vienna Woods to hunt for the Waldmeister. To me it looked just like cow parsley, and I am sure that is what I picked and brought back in large and smelly bunches. But although we awoke next morning to pounding hangovers, none of us was ever poisoned. And Ross purred for days after, at the thought of having been able to give his friends a genuine Waldmeister feast.

In our moments of leisure, Gretl and I swopped language lessons. I was helping her to perfect her English, while she endeavoured to hammer some German into my head. As everybody you ever met always firmly spoke English, it was difficult to get a chance to practise. I battled on, but it wasn't until I had to cope with a household staff, that I really began to speak. And then, although better than nothing, it was mostly kitchen German. This shortcoming led me into a trap, at least on one occasion. The German-speaking races always referred to their stay in prisoner-of-war camps as having been in KZ, short for Konzentration-slage. When the time came for me to engage a butler for my newly set-up married establishment, and I quizzed him on his past life, he informed me that he had been in KZ. As practically everyone in those parts had suffered the same fate, it seemed perfectly normal. Making sympathetic noises, I probed no further.

Came the time when a Polish officer, who was in charge of the radio station in the British Zone, paid us a few days' visit with his wife. Within twenty-four hours, their entire cash reserves had vanished from their luggage. Much distressed, I informed the Polizei, who, moving in for the day, took over the flat, turned everything upside down and fingerprinted everybody on the premises. As mine were being taken in the dining-room, the prisoner-butler, serving morning coffee and displaying disapproval, clucked with concern at the thought of anyone playing such a dirty trick upon me. By the end of the day, and to everybody's surprise, it was *he* who turned out to be the thief. The night before, he had gone out with the loot, all of which had been spent on a great blow-out for his ex-prisoner friends. When I expressed astonishment at his roguery, he pointed out, quite rightly, that he had told the truth at the interview, and that it was up to me to find out the kind of prison he was talking about.

As a cool customer he took some beating. Once back inside, re-installed in his KZ, great bundles of his prison trousseau used to arrive on the doorstep for the maid's attention, as the laundry service of his establishment didn't come up to scratch. And since the cuisine wasn't up to standard either, we were earnestly requested to deliver food parcels as well.

Gretl's adventures as a reporter on our German newspaper were numerous and picturesque. When Malcolm Sargent paid us a visit, it fell to her lot to attend his Press Conference. Having had a copious business lunch, she arrived late through no fault of her own, then promptly fell asleep. Waking up suddenly at question time, and wanting to make her mark and show she was on the ball, she piped up in her best English, 'Tell me, Sargent Malcolm,' but never got any further, the rest of the question being drowned by the hoots of laughter of the other Pressmen present. As winter progressed and the weather continued to grow colder, when on night duty, she would change into her nightdress in the office, where a fairly warm temperature was maintained, then, under the nose of the startled night porter, would beetle off into the snow in her nightgear, making for her icy flat as fast as she could, jumping straight into bed when she got there.

The thermometer dropped to thirty degrees below zero. People sometimes dropped dead in the street, frozen to the spot. As you couldn't hope to keep any skin on your face at that temperature in the mountains, all skiing had been abandoned. The snow now rose to the level of the first floor in the streets, and one fine day, to cheer ourselves up, we decided to give a party. Shortly before, we had managed to acquire a couple of electric fires of lethal design, made of painted pinewood, and equipped with a bar apiece. If we were lucky, and no one in the building was using a vacuum cleaner or an electric iron when we plugged in our fires, all was well. But more often than not, the entire fuse system of the building would blow up, and the infuriated inmates of the other flats congregated on our doorstep, cursing these bloody Englanders, who caused nothing but trouble.

The evening of our party, plugging in fortunately took place without incident, and we were able to raise the temperature in the flat by one or two degrees. I was busy chipping the frozen limejuice out of its bottle with a knitting needle, in order to melt it down on the gas as soon as this came on, when suddenly a wild demented banging on the front door made me jump out of my skin. Gretl was standing there in a great state of agitation. 'There's a Russian soldier in our flat,' she panted. 'What shall I do? We're all terrified ...'

'Hold on,' I said, dropping the bottle, 'I will ring the Military Police.' As these gentlemen assured me they would be round in a jiffy, we galloped upstairs, hoping that the sight of my uniform would act as a deterrent to whatever the Russian was plotting. There he was, standing in the middle of the kitchen, with his tommy-gun on the table, bemused and lost-looking, while all the Pippins were hiding under the beds.

'Engliski,' I announced in my best Russian, and pointing at my battledress jacket, 'What do you want?' Whereupon we were treated to a verbal flood of which we didn't catch a single word. There we were, all three standing around helplessly, when the Military Police, good as their word, arrived on the scene.

'Okay, girls, we'll take over,' they said soothingly, as they led the unprotesting youth away. It turned out, after all, that suddenly feeling like a cup of cocoa, he had wandered into the building, and rapped with the butt-end of his gun on the first door which took his fancy.

After this little excitement was over, we realised that time was flying. Gretl and the other Pippins, now coming out of hiding, offered to help with preparations for the party. The gas by now having flickered briefly and gone off again, had been switched off at the mains. And here was our limejuice, standing up solid as a rock, inside its bottle. Ingenious and practical as ever, Gretl tipped one of the fires on its back and upon its single bar, placed the saucepan, into which we quickly dropped the icicles chipped off the main iceberg and the situation was saved. Greatly relieved, we treated our chilblains to a quick warm-through, when all of a sudden a loud rap on the door made us jump to our feet.

'Heavens, not the guests already!' I exclaimed, making for the entrance. On the mat stood a couple of soldiers, this time our own, surrounded by crates and boxes of food.

'Good God,' I squeaked, horrified, 'it's the Russians!' Wednesday was Ration Day, when the Quartermaster, using our flat as a distribution centre for all the British officers living in the area, unloaded the stuff on us. Olive, with her Northern accent, pronounced rations as Russians, so that all of us, with one accord, followed her example without even thinking about it, which generally resulted in a certain amount of confusion.

In the living-room, poor Gretl started to tremble all over again, 'Noch einmal!' (Not again!) I heard her exclaim in alarm.

'It's all right,' I shouted; 'it's only the rations. Please come in,' and I led the way into the kitchen. At this point Olive, returning from the office, erupted into the kitchen. 'Oh my God, it's the Russians tonight! I forgot all about it.' Within a few minutes, and just before the party, our tiny kitchen was overflowing with groceries, great lumps of old Danish cow and New Zealand ram, and tins of jam and golden syrup, frozen solid like amber. 'We should have remembered the Russians were coming tonight,' Olive grumbled, as she went to her room to change. 'We should never have had that party on the same night!'

Since I had nothing to wear, Gretl lent me a flame-coloured organza dress, all heaving and bouncing with detached floating panels. Never in my life had I ever had anything so beautiful on my back. And had the party been a total flop, I would still have enjoyed the evening on account of that dress.

The Pippins' boyfriends had constructed a false ceiling of wire mesh, nice and low, which they covered with multi-coloured crepe paper, through which the electric bulb on the ceiling glowed dark red and lurid, as in a really sleazy dive.

I presume it was a good party, since nobody went home until morning. By nine o'clock, after Olive, green-faced and still grumbling about the Russians all over the kitchen, had tottered off to work, I picked up a broom and, still clad in the beautiful floating panels, began to clear up the mess. Alexander Bethune, who had gone home to shave, returned to find me hard at it. 'How about a cup of coffee for Cinderella?' he thoughtfully suggested. Having changed back regretfully into my drab khaki uniform, and half asleep on my feet, I stumbled off to the Mess with him for a late but welcome breakfast.

Although I was apparently not *due* for any leave, the Colonel nevertheless granted me a few days off, when I heard that my father was being sent home from Singapore by the Red Cross. My mother had already returned from Australia with Anne and Christine, and together we went to Victoria Station to meet his train. Looking up and down the rows of stunned, bemused prisoners, we could not spot him anywhere. In the end, I asked a policeman who, amazingly, led me straight to him. At the time, it never occurred to me to wonder how he could possibly have known my father. In the topsy-turvy world of the last few years, anything was possible, and you took what came your way without asking questions.

He looked unfamiliar, diminished, and frighteningly thin. He and his fellow prisoners had only just been rescued in time. For the last few months, they had been forced at gunpoint to dig tunnels, into which they would be herded, doused with petrol, and burnt to death if any Allied landings took place in Singapore. The first atom bomb had been dropped on Hiroshima on 6 August, and the world was stunned to hear that nearly one hundred thousand people were annihilated by one bomb. The resulting outcry of appalled indignation which rocked humanity did it credit, but it should be remembered that these courteous people, who bowed to one another all day long, also tortured their prisoners in an unbelievably atrocious way. An American naval commander whom I only recently met, is still in constant pain on account of the attentions he received from his gentle captors, while his men, who were taken prisoner at the same time, had their genitals sliced off and pegged up on a washing line for all to see. There is no doubt that human nature undergoes a fiendish change in times of war. Perfectly normal, well-meaning, kindly people, swop their souls with the Devil's own, and do his bidding with a kind of eager, mesmerised alacrity. The only way to protect ourselves and others from this seemingly inevitable and monstrous fate, is TO HAVE NO MORE WARS.

My mother had booked us all into a grim and depressing hotel in South Kensington, and there we gathered in the hideous lounge, making polite conversation.

Anne, who had trained as a nurse in Australia, was informed on arriving in England that she would have to start again from scratch, if she wanted to practise in the UK. She told me of their last nightmare days in Singapore, under intense Japanese bombardment, and a fearful thunderstorm, all crashing simultaneously around the sky, so that you couldn't tell a clap of thunder from an exploding bomb. Staying with friends while waiting to join the last refugee boat in the harbour, they had seen with their own eyes an incandescent ball of fire sweep in through the window, and roll slowly along the floor between their feet, then calmly out to the verandah to rejoin the chaos outside. On the way back from Australia, they had taken three months to zigzag across the Indian Ocean, and sail round the Cape, to be finally abandoned halfway by their convoy, who galloped on ahead at twice the speed which their old cargo was able to squeeze out of its antiquated engines. The ships disappearing over the horizon, left behind a feeling of utter desolation, which was reinforced the next day when a rowing-boat, seemingly empty, came floating towards them. Suspecting a Japanese booby-trap, they scrutinised it cautiously before approaching any closer. But it turned out to be a genuine case of survivors, only just still alive from a boat torpedoed and sunk in the area a couple of weeks earlier. And although, at great danger to itself, the little cargo tarried a couple of days, searching around for other survivors, nobody else remained on the surface of the unfriendly sea.

Christine, who was a lively sixteen-year-old, and feeling she ought to be doing something useful, had written off to the Admiralty, saying that she was thinking of becoming Captain of a warship, and would be happy to have one assigned to her as soon as possible. A courteous reply came from their Lordships, regretting that, at the moment, there were no vacancies for young ladies in top-ranking appointments in the Royal Navy. But they would keep her in mind, and inform her as soon as something suitable turned up. Although she didn't know it at the time, she was by no means the first female to apply for a post of this kind. A Chelsea resident, Miss Chamberlayne, 'Aspiring above her sex and age,' to quote the official records, joined her brother's ship, and went through a battle against the French in 1690, dressed and armed like a man.

But in spite of toiling and moiling to renew the old family ties, after so many years of separation, we were strangers to one another. The atmosphere, stiff and strained, amazed me. I never thought that this moment, which I had looked forward to so much, and for such a long time, when we would swop tales of our adventures and misfortunes, and rejoice together at still being alive after it all, could be such a painful experience. My father, who had never been exactly intimate with anyone in his life, and who had withdrawn still further into himself since his ordeal in the concentration camp, was obviously longing to get away from us all.

After a few days of this disappointing get-together, I felt guiltily relieved to return to Vienna, to the unexacting, problem-free existence to which I had now become addicted. My last day was spent in Harrods, buying shoes and heavy winter clothes, and great quantities of glass balls for a really first-class Christmas tree.

It took over forty-eight hours to get back by military train through Holland and Germany. We stopped at railside depots at regular intervals, for meals and showers, and everywhere snow lay in huge great drifts, mountains of it, on both sides of the train. In Vienna, the cold was more bitter than ever, and lorries, piled high with dirty snow scooped up from the streets, were driving off in convoy to dump their load onto the ice-floes of the frozen Danube.

Among the commissions and gifts for various friends with which I had returned from London, was a hefty parcel for a family of young Austrians, whose aunt I had met in London. Thinking they would come and collect their loot from my office, I rang them up on arrival, but they insisted I should deliver it in person, so that I could see for myself how destitute they truly were. To my surprise, I found a jolly, high-spirited, well-dressed crowd of people clustered round an enormous porcelain stove, reaching up to the ceiling. The room, a good deal warmer than any of our messes or requisitioned hotels, was in no way to be compared with the deep-freeze conditions in which I lived in my little flat. As I expressed genuine surprise, they exclaimed indignantly, 'But we have lost everything! The Russians have taken everything away, furniture, clothes, pictures, all we had. We are very, very poor.' Having said their piece, and as they paid no more attention to me, I got up to leave. To my surprise at such a display of English manners, one of the young men sprang up, and opened the door for me. 'I'll walk you back to your hotel,' he said gallantly.

'Please don't bother. I'm going to the office anyway.'

'That will do just as well.' And taking me by the arm, he steered me expertly through the frozen ruts of the street.

'How do you come to speak such good English?' I asked, more and more puzzled.

'I had an English nanny.'

'Oh, did you! And where is she now?' I asked, thinking of the horrors of the Bolzano concentration camp.

'Just been liberated. She was interned during the war, poor old dear. But now she is back at our place in Carinthia.'

'I'm so glad. And now, this is my office, thank you for seeing me back.'

'I'll collect you for lunch tomorrow,' he said, and to my surprise, he did.

After that, I was often invited to stay at 'our place in Carinthia', a Gothic castle built on top of a perpendicular peak near the Jugoslav frontier. Like so many Austrian families, and although their possessions had been decimated, they appeared to live in great comfort, compared with my own ice-bound way of life. Their vast estates provided plenty of firewood for the huge porcelain stoves, while roast duck and poultry, venison, capercailzie, trout from their own stream, and all sorts of other delicacies, appeared at every meal. To one who had been living on army field rations for the last two years, this was like visiting another planet. If it hadn't been for the constant plaints of the older generation, who moaned incessantly that they had lost everything, it would have been hard to remember that there had been a war at all. Another thing which took me time to get used to, was having my hand kissed by the maids every time they came into my bedroom.

We spent the weekend skiing with an enormous collection of cousins, and in the evening we danced in the vast stone-floored hall, the walls of which were lined to the rafters with generations of stuffed chamois heads. Although my school German was beginning to improve, there was little chance to practise it, as they all spoke excellent English.

The parties with which ACA celebrated Christmas, were very different from the year before. The Colonel's driver and I toiled off to the Vienna Woods to seek out the biggest and finest tree which we could manage to bring back. Decorated with all my glass balls from Harrods, it was the centre of the festivities and rejoicings which took place in the Mess. The first Christmas since the end of the war was celebrated with an impressive number of atom bombs, and a couple of stringy little turkeys, no doubt captured in the wilds of our Zone, by the Quartermaster's minions.

The Kinsky Palace, requisitioned as a British Officers' Club, held a great Boxing Day feast, at which Max Wilde and I disgraced ourselves by galloping tipsily round the ballroom, while everybody else was dancing sedately cheek-to-cheek. Then there was a ponderous cocktail party at the Embassy, where a stampede took place for the small eats, which were cleaned up within a few minutes by the Austrian guests present. There was another tough turkey feast at the Park Hotel, and the rest of the holiday was spent trying to keep warm in Sacher's bar.

When all these festivities were over and our usual routine was resumed, the normal life of the city gradually began to get on its feet again. Concerts, opera and the theatre emerged from their long sleep with a new vigour, and we went to practically everything. As I understood but little German, I found the theatre a crashing bore, and when I did get the drift of what was going on, I couldn't really change my mind. Earnest and pompous, the plays we saw at that time had nothing to recommend them. The only memorable one was *Anna Karenina*, with Hilde

Wagner, the senior actress of the Burgtheater, in the lead. Hilde became a great friend, and later married, with qualified success, one of our officers.

The concerts and the opera were a great joy. Elizabeth Schwarzkopf and Ljuba Welitsch sang Mozart. Karajan frequently conducted the Vienna Philharmonic, as well as Kripps and Klemperer, a terrible old goat who pinched all the bottoms within his reach. There was an artist's restaurant, all upholstered in red plush like the old Café Royal, where we met all these characters after the evening's performances. A great treat for late supper was Fogosch, a delicious fish from Lake Balaton in Hungary, and secretly brought into Vienna by the engine-driver of the night train from Buda-Pest. The headwaiter, full of pomp and circumstance, would come up, announcing importantly, 'Der Schmugler ist da. Do you wish Fogosch tonight?' And of course, since the smuggler was there with his Fogosch, we had to have it, however expensive it might be.

Finally, the winter was drawing to an end. As the last of the snow disappeared and the sun was gathering heat, and the smell of spring was in the air, I approached the Colonel in fear and trepidation.

'I would like to go to Prague,' I informed him. 'I want to see Czechoslovakia before it is too late.'

'Good idea,' he answered to my surprise. 'A few days in Prague would be very interesting. In fact I wouldn't mind going to have a look at it myself.'

This was more than I would have dared hope for. And so, as a result, it was all done in the greatest comfort available at the time. We had a sleeper each, all very correct, with a connecting door which opened in the morning to make a large and spacious compartment. From dawn onward I was glued to the window not wanting to miss a thing. With its narrow streams and tumbling waterfalls, and sharp craggy peaks, it was all true Zenda country.

From time to time, a Gothic castle carved out of the rock flashed by, or a chamois, alarmed by the racket of our train, leapt over a crevice. The thick dense forest, almost black, which covered every inch of the ground, had probably never been cleared since the beginning of time. Prague, which is in the heart of Bohemia, and which had been fairly knocked about during the war, was a curious mixture of dusty dirt streets and massive, impressive, and rather gloomy medieval buildings. The Charles Bridge, with its rows of saints mounting guard on either side, and which dates from the fourteenth century, had been mercifully spared, as well as the fortified town of Hradčany, the seat of the Dukes of Bohemia, on the other side of the river.

The day after our arrival, the streets filled with people, and in the middle of the morning, an enormous cavalcade of tanks and gun-carriers came rattling down the road. Marshal Tito, standing to attention in an open jeep, was on his way back from Poland, where he had been paying an official visit.

The Czechs, a people of strong feelings, were unpredictable in their reactions. The previous day they had spat on the ground before answering our questions in German, the only language we had in common. Now it seemed we were no longer so popular. Perhaps Tito's friends outnumbered the patriots, but whatever the reason, our British Army uniforms were definitely unappreciated. Feeling *de trop*, we retired to our hotel. At the Shrubek, where we were staying, the atmosphere was eerie and unreal, filled with British businessmen whose activities had been suspended, and who were forbidden to practise their calling, presumably pending a decision about the future of Czechoslovakia. The situation was very confused. The Russians, who were on the brink but had made no open move as yet, were regarded, rather naively, by the Czechs as 'Big Brother Slav'.

The following day, the last of our stay, and wanting to

see something of the countryside, we took a train to the south, chugging past a great many more craggy castles guarding lonely mountain passes on the way. Getting out in the middle of Moravia, we walked for miles in the lovely wooded countryside. In the end, totally lost, we called at a lonely farmhouse, and there were offered a feast of black bread and freshly boiled EGGS! The first we had tasted since the beginning of the war. That was an egg I shall never forget. But it was growing dark, and we had to find our way back to Prague. The farmer drove us to the station in a horse-drawn cart, and as there was probably only one train in the area, it got us back to Prague, in the pitch dark of its unlit streets.

On my return from Prague, I found I had been transferred to the British *Morning News* office. In a daily paper, there was actually something to show for your work, whereas on the Newsdesk, your stuff, which you never saw again, just disappeared into limbo, and might for all you knew never be used at all.

John Cox (he of the Pippins), as the Editor, ruled over a neat and orderly office of half a dozen journalists, who were kept by him in a constant state of gloom and despondency. He detested the breed and all they stood for, feared their irreverence, and distrusted the cheerful inconsequence of their ways. As a result, all dash and glamour having gone out of their work, they toiled reluctantly in sullen silence under his sway. A news office, he used to say, should be run like a greengrocer's shop. Inscrutable as a Buddha, he sat at his desk, upon which you couldn't even see a paper clip. The copy, as soon as it was rushed in, still warm from the teleprinters, was stored away in his drawers to cool its heels there until all the excitement of a red-hot piece of news had evaporated into thin air. Then, and only then, it was doled out to us in his soft whispery voice. The writer who was summoned, had to go to the desk to collect his work, just like trotting up to the teacher at school. If anyone was bold enough to stand up and stretch his legs, or hiss a few curses into his neighbour's ear, John would breathe at once, 'What's the matter? Are you stuck? Do you want a dictionary?' These were kept locked up in the filing cabinet behind his desk, and handed out on request.

In the morning, Cobby, a real hard-bitten pro from Fleet Street, tottered into the office an hour late, swaying in on her high-heeled rickety sandals, with enormous round holes in her fishnet stockings, and bright orange-coloured powder spread in great irregular streaks across her face. 'Good evening, boys and girls,' she croaked, before John had time to remark on the lateness of the hour. Then she picked up the copy on her table and began to poke about on the keyboard. 'Damn typewriter keeps jumping about,' she muttered. 'Darling, be a love and give me a cigarette, and for Christ's sake, Cox, stop looking at me like that!' And I fished out a cigarette and lit it for her. 'Thanks, darling, that's much better. Now let's see what we've got here.' And her professionalism would carry her through the worst part of her hangover, until mercifully released by the lunch hour, when she clattered round to the Mess as fast as she could for a reviving gin and tonic.

Escaping on the dot of one, the others followed her to the bar, to recover from the strain of the morning, and to complain bitterly about the unnatural and undignified treatment to which they were subjected. Colonel Beau-clerk, who was firm, but just and sympathetic, mixing and joking and drinking with everybody, listened to their complaints and explained the reason for things as they were, and why they had to be. Quite soon, restored by their favourite tipple and their own witticisms, they had forgotten their troubles, and all resentment evaporated under the influence of the Colonel's infectious optimism.

Owing to his personality and talent for knitting together people of different social and intellectual levels, it was a happy Mess, with a minimum of intrigue and malicious gossip. Life was also more predictable, now that the Americans were no longer with us. I must admit that I missed their flamboyant extravagance. Nothing with them was ever impossible. Their working methods, and their picturesque turn of phrase, had been a stimulating experience. Now, life was more earnest, though only by comparison with an American Mess. The view taken at the top was that as long as people did their job, their private life was their own affair, and the usual drinking and fornicating flourished uninterrupted, and as happily as ever without blame or reproof of any kind.

Cobby, who was the life and soul of the journalists' world, held court every evening in Sacher's bar, where any man around was irresistibly drawn to her table by her husky voice, her infectious chuckling, her vitality, and the boldness and lewdness of her conversation. As drinks came and went, the party grew in size and boisterousness until, around nine o'clock, she would totter to her feet and lead her chaps, tight as ticks, into the dining-room for dinner. Her parties, which often lasted all night, were very popular. I was never invited, but Alexander, who was an habitué, often described them, explaining that she only carried on in this way because she had but three months left to live. Ten years later, when I saw her again, she was still as hale and indefatigable as ever, having lost none of her vivacity, her charm, or her magnetism.

My little Austrian baron, at whose place in Carinthia I often stayed, and whose name was Bobby, had invited me to open the New Year's Eve Ball with him in Vienna. This tradition, which has survived the war and continues to this day to be one of the main social functions of the season, gets the New Year off with a bang. The girls, all decked out in virginal white, line up with their escorts round the edge of the enormous ballroom, and at the first note of the *Blue Danube*, sail off in one huge spinning garland of rustling, flying white. I was much looking forward to this lark.

Idly chatting in Sacher's bar one evening, and thinking nothing of it, I informed the Colonel of my New Year's plans, adding that Bobby's nanny was kindly sewing me a white dress for the occasion. To my surprise, he was most indignant.

'Certainly not,' he said firmly. 'There is no question of your going to the New Year's Eve Ball with an Austrian. You will join my party in the ISB box. It has all been arranged, and nothing can be changed now.' And the subject was closed.

Bobby, who was furious when I told him, lectured me at great length on the frivolity of my ways, and my disgraceful behaviour. Going out with a different man every night could not possibly do my reputation any good. Laughing in his face, I informed him that I didn't give a damn for my 'reputation', who had ever heard of such a thing anyway, and that I would go out with whoever I pleased at all times, and that no man would ever boss me around or curtail my freedom. Anyone who tried to do that, I declared, staring him pointedly in the eye, became an inveterate bore. Independence and freedom of action, I informed him haughtily, were what mattered to me most in the world.

Brave words. A year later, matrimony having caught up with me, I willingly surrendered my precious, much-vaunted freedom, and for the first time in my life, I began to consider my appearance, and to deplore the shortcomings of nature. Scrutinising the features of the girls around me, I began to register envy, a new and uncomfortable kind of feeling I didn't like at all. How was it, I wondered despondently, that I seemed to be the only Plain Jane among them?

But, as the Americans would say, so dumb was I that

the possibility of make-up having anything to do with their dazzling looks, never even crossed my mind. Still less did it occur to me to experiment with it myself. Since I assumed that nothing could be done about the matter, I deliberately and resolutely decided to forget all about it, and set out to make the most of my new existence. Beauty or no beauty, married life, if I had anything to say in the matter, was going to be fun.